ADVANCE PRAISE FOR

GENERATIVE KNOWING: PRINCIPLES, METHODS AND DISPOSITIONS OF AN EMERGING ADULT LEARNING THEORY

"With cascading words, images, stories and meanings, and courageous vulnerability, Nicolaides weaves a phenomenological and DeLeuzian portrait of generative knowing that is both generative and phenomenal. The artistic use of language and story to look at how we come to know in the face of unprecedented complexity and ambiguity brings poetry to scholarship. Scholars of adult learning will recognize the power of this contribution to evolving adult learning theory. This book will be a classic among adult learning scholars."

Karen E. Watkins, Professor
Learning, Leadership and Organizational Development,
The University of Georgia

"Overwhelmed and frequently shocked by the complexity, turbulence, and velocity of our lived experience today, haven't we all stopped to wonder, how will we find a constructive way forward? Nicolaides' stunning contribution to the field is an invitation to feel our way forward by growing new senses and new sensibilities. *Generative Knowing* is not an easy quick fix, but it is a summons to discover "the door in every moment" to try something new, in our ways of being, relating, our ways of leading, and organizing ourselves. Reading it, I feel grounded and yet hopeful for what is waiting to emerge through us and our collective action."

Rev. David C. McCallum, S.J., Ed.D
Executive Director, Program for Discerning Leadership

"Aliki Nicolaides' masterpiece, *Generative Knowing: Principles, Methods and Dispositions of an Emerging Adult Learning Theory*, itself emerges from her own, her mother's and her father's lifetimes of literal nomadic experiences, yanking them from their Greek-Palestinian roots, to decades in Singapore, and then more decades in the U.S. Through painful revelations, she illustrates a theory and practice of nomadic learning for generative knowing. This practice cuts below the fog of cultural assumptions and traumatic forgetfulness—below learning for doing and learning for knowing—to learning for being and becoming. As our global society roller coasters toward rapidly increasing refugee dislocations, as well as pandemic, climatological, political, and economic disruptions, Nicolaides' approach to learning will resonate for more and more of us."

William R. Torbert
Leadership Professor Emeritus, Boston College
Author of Numbskull in the Theatre of Inquiry: Transforming Self, Friends, Organizations, and Social Science

"Aliki takes the conversation on adult learning to a much-needed new level. In reading this book one has an opportunity for understanding learning from a different perspective and to reflect on one's own potential for insights drawn from one's unawareness of how learning is influenced at the subconscious level. Based on a foundation of philosophies, multiple ontologies, and rich descriptions of Aliki's personal experiences, this book provides a way into learning from experience existing beneath one's awareness. I believe *Generative Knowing* is a necessary read for adult learning professionals and others as we enter an age of increasing ambiguity."

Dr. Lyle Yorks, Professor Emeritus
Teachers College, Columbia University, New York

"A brilliant illustration through personal biography of articulating the intra-connectedness of reality in experience heretofore communicable largely via presentational knowing. An enactment of Eliot's poignant, 'The trilling wire in the blood/Sings below inveterate scars'—embracing ambiguity, pushing beyond the limits of a quest for certainty!"

Victoria J. Marsick, Ph.D.
Academic Director, Adult Learning & Leadership
Department of Organization & Leadership, Teachers College,
Columbia University

"The deceptive simplicity of ordinary words is harnessed by Aliki Nicolaides in this fascinating book in which she weaves a rich tapestry of adult learning theory. Through the variety of the warp and weft, a story emerges that gives full expression to the possibilities of adult learning. From East to West and through rich life experiences each strand is given its moment to shine and dance to become in the book a colourful woven tapestry of lifelong learning – eloquent, insightful, and unique."

Dr. Ted Fleming, Associate Professor
Maynouth University, National University of Ireland, Maynouth

"This remarkable book is a call to action for the field of adult learning. Dr. Nicolaides models a response to this challenge by developing a robust theory of 'generative knowing as ways of being and becoming, actualizing potential creatively by poking fissures of light in the territory beneath living experience.' These fissures of light that she sheds on her own personal and family histories beautifully illuminate the entanglement of phenomenology, new materialisms, and embodied learning. Through this journey she beautifully and convincingly constructs a 'nomadic theory of adult learning' - a way forward during these chaotic, ambiguous times toward more inclusive and just futures."

Dr. Trena Paulus
Professor, Qualitative Methodologist & Research Technologist
East Tennessee State, Johnson City, Tennessee, USA

GENERATIVE KNOWING

GENERATIVE KNOWING

~ Principles, Methods, and Dispositions of an Emerging Adult Learning Theory

BY ALIKI NICOLAIDES

Gorham, Maine

Copyright © 2023 | Myers Education Press, LLC
Published by Myers Education Press, LLC
P.O. Box 424
Gorham, ME 04038

All rights reserved. No part of this book may be reprinted or reproduced in any form or by any electronic, mechanical, or other means, now known or hereafter invented, including photocopying, recording, and information storage and retrieval, without permission in writing from the publisher.

Myers Education Press is an academic publisher specializing in books, e-books and digital content in the field of education. All of our books are subjected to a rigorous peer review process and produced in compliance with the standards of the Council on Library and Information Resources.

Library of Congress Cataloging-in-Publication Data available from Library of Congress.

13-digit ISBN 978-1-9755-0399-4 (paperback)
13-digit ISBN 978-1-9755-0400-7 (library networkable e-edition)
13-digit ISBN 978-1-9755-0401-4 (consumer e-edition)

Printed in the United States of America.

All first editions printed on acid-free paper that meets the American National Standards Institute Z39-48 standard.

Books published by Myers Education Press may be purchased at special quantity discount rates for groups, workshops, training organizations and classroom usage. Please call our customer service department at 1-800-232-0223 for details.

Cover design by Teresa Lagrange Design Service from Portland, ME
Cover Artwork by David Holmes

David is an award-winning American artist whose work is exhibited worldwide. His photorealistic paintings depict modern urban life and explore themes of culture, status and gentrification. www.holmespaint.com

Visit us on the web at **www.myersedpress.com** to browse our complete list of titles.

Dedication

For Yiayia Kostandia, who knit us together even when we were distanced by land, sea, and the different cultures our nomadic lives brought us to. For the lineage of women who continue to live through me. For the devoted fathers, grandfathers, brothers, and uncles who made house and home many times over. For deep connected friendships that make love real. Big love!

Contents

List of Figures	xi
Acknowledgments	xiii
Foreword	xv
Prologue	xxi
ONE Generative Knowing: A Nomadic Theory of Adult Learning	1
TWO A Brief Review of Adult Learning Theory	13
THREE Following the Phenomenon in Phenomenological Research	29
FOUR Luminous Darkness	51
FIVE A Single Story is a Dangerous Narrative	63
SIX Mother Nature: Signals from a Different Plane	85
SEVEN Generative Knowing & the Future of Work *Ahreum Lim*	103
EIGHT The Dynamics of Generative Learning	129
About the Authors	137
Index	139

List of Figures

Figure 5.1: The Most Beautiful Woman in Jerusalem — 64

Figure 5.2: Three Musketeers — 65

Figure 5.3: Martha Committed to Singapore's Becoming — 68

Figure 5.4: Martha Featured in Singapore-Based Magazines and Newspapers — 75

Figure 6.1: Young Aristotle — 91

Figure 6.2: Aristotle from 1946 to 1948 — 93

Figure 6.3: The Mortar Bombing — 95

Figure 6.4: Ari Being Young Adult — 97

Figure 7.1: A Collage of Photos of My Dad Working in the Company — 110

Figure 7.2: A Collage of Photos Showing my Mom Working in the Corporation — 111

Acknowledgments

THIS IS MY BOOK. I cannot say that I wrote this book alone. That would be untrue. What is true for me is that this book is filled with many truths, the mystery of my being and becoming, and the freedom to offer knowing that is a grace given. The book is a living inquiry with myself, with the people I love, and the love people give in mutual and spontaneous ways. People need people.

This book would not have become a book without the people who saw that there is truth, mystery, and beauty in what wants to be written by my hand. I have learned that I have a rhythm deep inside me that is much slower, quiet, shy, and in touch with the sensations of disquieting times. These are times in which to listen. To receive. To reach out and trust that together we can learn to creatively find a way to make new worlds with us. To act together and be different is a potent mystery we must learn to harness. Thank you for reading my book, a book that took generations to make.

My gratitude extends to the veranda of my maternal grandmother's apartment in Greece, where so many stories were told and my story was listened to. My Yiayia Costandia listened first, may her memory be eternal. I extend my deep gratitude to Martha and Ari, my parents and now housemates. Thank you for allowing me to listen to your stories differently and share them. Thank you to my beloved siblings, Katia and Theo, who trusted that the stories I would tell would transform our lineage from the snags on which it was caught. Thank you, my sister cousin, Ilene, who never doubted I could write this book. And thank you, Shakiyla, my twin in the deep dark waters of being and becoming, who read my early chapters with such care and devotion. I love and adore you. Thank you David, my beloved lifelong friend, for accompanying me these past 18 years into the dark, hand in hand. I want to thank the thought leaders who never hesitated when I shared with them that "I am going to write a book." Lyle Yorks, Karen Watkins, Victoria Marsick, and Bill Torbert said they could not wait to read it and encouraged me every time that courage deserted me during these past two years.

What would I do without the "accompanists," my brood of soulful friends who span lifetimes of inquiry around the world? Each of them accompanied me just when I needed them. Trena and David, who offered me their home in Johnson City, TN, where I could write in the warmth of their hospitality when it was really cold outside. Ruth, who walked this book with me, hearing every twist and turn of self-doubt and shy excitement. Andrea, who has become family. Joanne Yorks, whom I thank for reading chapters of my book when I panicked. Dyan Holt, my Singaporean-Athens (GA) friend, who has read this book in the making many times. I am so grateful for your editorial support.

There are three more unique relationships for which I want to express gratitude. To Ahreum Lim, author of one chapter in my book, graduate student who arrived in the United States just months before the pandemic went wild. Ahreum has been with me in this writing from the start: writing with me, thinking with me, and trusting that what I was showing her was going to create spaces of possibility for her being and becoming. A deep bow to you, Ahreum. I love you. Elizabeth Kasl and I have become thinking companions. I was so shy in asking her to read my book as I was writing it; in asking her to share her thoughts, feelings, and resonances stirred by her reading; in asking the matriarch of my field of adult learning to write the foreword. Elizabeth, you are beautiful, generous, and deeply grounded in the evolution of adult learning. I prostrate myself before you in gratitude.

There is one more special person to thank. The pandemic ravaged the world, breaking it open and allowing for light to enter dark places that, now illuminated, are stirring new worlds into being, worlds we could not foreknow. One fissure that opened unexpectedly was the shy longing for intimate companionship. Surprisingly, a loving companion found me. I am hard to find, it turns out. Cecil found me. I am so grateful that you saw me first. Big love!

Foreword

ALIKI NICOLAIDES IS A PROMINENT leader among adult education scholar-practitioners who have shaped the discourse about transformative learning, which is the context in which I have enjoyed coming to know her. At the 2012 International Transformative Learning Conference, several adult educators formed an intention to provide oversight and stewardship for future conferences. Our loosely organized group might not have persevered if Aliki had not stepped in to take on the task of providing much-needed leadership. I have watched with growing appreciation as I witness her vision, inclusive spirit, and grasp of organizational development in shepherding a group of busy academics, many of whom have been leaders in this field far longer than she has. Without her cheerful persistence and attention to detail, I think it likely that we would have failed to achieve the oversight goals we set for ourselves in 2012. Thus, it was with pleasure that I responded to her request to offer critical feedback about a book she was writing. With an equal measure of pleasure, I accept her invitation to write this foreword.

This book grows from the personhood of the Aliki I have come to appreciate. She tells us, "I have had this book in me for a long time, in that part of me that has been waiting for me to find the courage to write it . . . a book I have been imagining since I completed my doctoral dissertation in 2008." The book is filled with academic scholarship, as befits a book that has been "in" someone since completing the rigorous experience of doctoral research. Equally important, though, the book is grown from the rich soil of Aliki's lived experience. At its heart, in three chapters based on her personal biography and the biographies of her mother and father, the text describes how she has lived the theory she now offers.

Before Aliki began her doctoral studies in adult education, she was a practitioner involved in leadership development for young women in Southeast Asia. She describes her pedagogy: "In the programs I designed and facilitated, one of the ways I engaged the participants was to bring them close to the threshold of the unknown . . . . I could feel the inviting potential that was beneath the threat that ambiguity posed, where potential and a place for deep learning dwelt." With wry reflection she adds, "What I also found was that very few of the participants had the same level of enthusiasm as I did for the vital learning through the unknown that an experience of ambiguity brings." And so, Aliki returned to school to learn more about learning, culminating her doctoral education in dissertation research about the nature of "learning through ambiguity." That concept has grown "in" her and emerges in full flower as a learning theory about what she calls generative knowing, a way of knowing that is rooted in "the experience beneath experience." She defines generative knowing "as ways of being and becoming that activate potential creatively" and explains this activation as interrelated processes of rupturing, *In-scending*, and *Awaring*.

Before her account of how generative knowing with its activating processes resides in her personal biography, we are treated to a thorough grounding in scholarly discourse about the nature of experience and its relationship to learning, as well as the nature of ambiguity. She incorporates perspectives from the same wide range of disciplines that guided her dissertation research—"complexity science, quantum theory, constructive developmental theory, evolutionary biology, pragmatism, Buddhism . . . ." She reviews how key concepts in the theory—such as being, becoming, *Awaring*—are described in academic literature, as well as how the nature of the theory—nomadic—is similarly rooted. Finally, she creates a dialogue among differing perspectives about adult learning that are common in the adult education literature.

Because the theory's evolution is so deeply embedded in the theorist's biography, I think it is relevant to reflect on her character. In describing how I have come to know Aliki, I referred to her vision, inclusive spirit, and cheerful persistence. As I read her text, I found illustrations of other important personal characteristics. Here is one example: In the chapter that describes her phenomenological approach to creating this book, as well as her dissertation methodology, I encountered a passage that took my breath away—an excerpt from a conversation that was part of Aliki's dissertation research. She began her interviews with her research subjects by performing a short, three-act play that she wrote in order to initiate an exploratory conversation about ambiguity. It is to that play that the opening segment in the following excerpt refers. Alex, who is a described as a powerful white man, interrupts their conversation.

Foreword　　　　　　　　　　　　　　　　　　　　　　　　　　　　xvii

Alex: I am bored with our conversation at this moment. You must have more ways to engage me. What is the next act?

Researcher: I am not sure what you mean. What act?

Alex: Your performance intrigued and attracted me. This conversation does not. Forced ambiguity is a killer.

Researcher: My next act is to let you know that I am now afraid of you and intimidated by you. I feel shut down and simultaneously angry at your arrogance and voyeurism. I am not here to perform for you. WE are here in your home, amongst your things, in a place where you are in control, seeking the ambiguity that may arise in the space between us. At this moment I feel powerless and my shields are up!

Alex: Ah ha! Power.... I was wondering when that was going to come up. You took up your power so fully in your performance and yet here I experience you as awkward and want to assert my power. How might we restore a power between us?

Researcher: *Breathing deep a few times* ... feeling a little wobbly ... I need courage in this moment and I ask that you see how your power moves, in the moments before, were just that, power moves that come with privilege.

Alex: Well said and named. I accept my bad behavior and regret my initial stance. I see now that we need to drop into some mutual space. How?

Researcher: Can we sing a song together? How about row, row, row your boat?

We sing together and begin to laugh.

I wrote above that reading this passage "took my breath away." What did I mean? I was first startled and then profoundly appreciative. When Aliki describes her "next act," she identifies several different emotions in her reaction to Alex's interrupting commentary, offers analysis of the power differential between them, and concludes with a metaphor, "my shields are up." We see her demonstrate complexity of thought, quick-wittedness, courage, and integrity. When she suggests they sing "row, row, row your boat," she also shows intuitive knowing, creativity, and playfulness.

I chose this text because I think it illustrates many of Aliki's personal characteristics, but equally important, I chose it because of what it illustrates about the book's style and purpose. My personal experience with this passage relates to both: After recovering from my initial surprise when I read the passage, and pausing to admire Aliki's response, I thought about what I might have done had I been in Aliki's shoes. I am confident that I would not have had the presence of mind to identify the complex dynamics that she named, nor, if I did recognize them, the gumption to say them out loud to this powerful man. In the several days that have passed since I read the passage, I have returned many times to speculate about my own reaction: How would I have responded in body and mind? What would I have said? Or done? Might I have cried? What action might I have taken after the interview? And, more importantly, how are all of those responses still present in me as I live today? What does my experience with these reflections teach me now?

Aliki explains that my response is her intention. She advises her readers, "I invite you to read as an intentional practice: That as a reader, you continue to observe your own experience of reading and the sensations that arise through this process." She has written a book that is at heart phenomenological. Her descriptions of lived experiences provide portals through which readers can enter their own "experience beneath experience" and thus embody the theory of generative knowing.

Because so much of the book examines the dynamics of personal learning and coming to know, it is possible to lose sight of the assumption that change in individual consciousness is intertwined with societal change. That Aliki perceives education to be a path toward a more just and inclusive society is threaded throughout the text. I think her conceptualization of generative knowing may encounter a fate similar to Jack Mezirow's description of perspective transformation. Because the focus is on individual learning and change, it can be too easily overlooked that the author assumes a spiral of interaction between growth of individual consciousness and change in organizations and communities in which the individual has agency.

I bring this Foreword to a close with a brief preview of what it is like to walk with Aliki as she describes her vision about generative knowing. There is poetry in her prose. And, just as she used the metaphor of "shields" when she spoke with Alex, she uses metaphor and analogy to create a phenomenological field. Here are but a few examples:

"This book uncovers what I have encountered as I live and walk alongside this inquiry."

"Another decade has passed, and in spite of a decade more of playing with ambiguity, dressing it in costumes that appear easier to encounter than its own raw force, I find that I am disillusioned."

"I saw myself keeping one foot in the known and the other in the unknown (locked in-between two worlds). I was bound by a well-worn groove that was no longer so groovy."

"This book will illuminate generative knowing as ways of being and becoming, actualizing potential creatively by poking fissures of light in the territory beneath living experience."

"Adult learning as we know it has been defined, redefined, played with like Silly Putty made into so many different shapes . . . ."

This book is written for all of us who care passionately about the potential of education for adults. We are called to commit ourselves not only to fostering "learning that" and "learning how," but also to "learning to become."

I've been engaging with theory about adult learning since I was a graduate student in the early 1970s at Teachers College, Columbia University. While enrolled one semester in a small seminar called "How Adults Learn" with Jack Mezirow, I enjoyed being introduced to adult learning as he worked out his ideas about perspective transformation. For several years, I taught the course "How Adults Learn" in the Adult Education Guided Independent Studies (AEGIS) program that Mezirow founded at Teachers College before I moved to San Francisco to help create a PhD program in transformative learning at the California Institute of Integral Studies.

Over the course of my teaching career, I focused on collaborative learning, participatory inquiry, the role of diversity in knowledge construction, and holism in the learning process and in pedagogical practice. I helped create and participated actively in three small-group learning collaboratives: Group for Collaborative Inquiry, Transformative Learning Collaborative, and European-American Collaborative Challenging Whiteness. The last group was founded in 1997 and continues to this day. These collaboratives are both a location for members' learning and an actor in the public arena through writing and workshop facilitation. Using the name of the collaborative as author or facilitator in lieu of individual names is a political statement about how knowledge is constructed.

Elizabeth Kasl, Independent Scholar
March 29, 2022

Prologue

Ruptures

I COME FROM A LINE OF people who were displaced during the 1947–1949 Arab Israeli War fought in Palestine, known to Palestinians as the *Nabka* (catastrophe—referring to the ethnic cleansing of Palestine and the near destruction of Palestinian society in 1948); and the Six-Day War (June 5–10, 1967, a war fought between the Israelis and the coalition formed by Syria, Jordan, and Egypt). I am of Asia Minor Greek and Palestinian heritage. This means that I am of Asia Minor Greek parents whose roots in Palestine span more than 100 years, and spread across much geopolitical scarrings that mark the lands and people of Palestine (including my parents and extended family).

I am the firstborn of the first generation born on land other than Palestine, due to geopolitical messes I had nothing to do with. I was born in Indianapolis, Indiana, USA, and when I was four years old, I moved to the island of Crete and then Athens, Greece, for a total of six years. In 1979, my family moved to Singapore, where we lived for 21 years. These movements mirror the nomadic life of displaced people. I inherited the sensations of loss, fear, and survival that my parents endured as they were uprooted from the land of their home due to circumstances not of their own making. I am displaced and always longing to belong, a sensation I cannot shake, a sensation that is at the root of my living inquiry and the basis of this book. It is not lost upon me that as I write this book, a global pandemic rages on; everything I have relied on, including my voice, shakes, as I dare to write from the inside of sensations that quiver beneath my being, where my becoming has been slowly and intentionally awakening from an unnatural stillness that I thought I had to keep—a stillness I believed was the formula for staying safe and belonging. This unnatural stillness was tangled in the range of responses I enacted when I encountered the chaos of my life experiences. In the parts of my being where there was stillness, I discovered I have a fear that I cannot shake: that I will be left behind. It fuels my longing to belong, to be received, welcomed not as a stranger but as a special guest. The sensation of stillness is like that of a little girl who finds herself in a room full of rare and beautiful things that can break easily with too much movement or by jumping for joy. My natural state is fire, the fire that comes from being the firstborn of displaced parents whose lives were ruled by forces of fear, loss, and survival, arrested in a perpetual seeking for rest and hospitality. My curiosity about the sensation of (un)natural stillness has guided many inquiries that have resulted in uncovering a different form of learning that I call generative knowing. It is the subject of this book.

In 2003, I returned to higher education to pursue a doctorate in adult learning and leadership. Prior to that, for the first decade of my work, these two concepts—learning and leadership—had dominated my approach to designing programs to foster young women's leadership capacity in Southeast Asia, where I grew up and lived. In those days I designed and facilitated learning programs that integrated ideas informed by developmental psychology, learning science, theories and practices of leadership development, and the tools of conflict resolution. These creations were based on my education as a political scientist and student of Gandhian Satyagraha in the then-nascent field of conflict resolution.

In the programs I designed and facilitated, one of the ways I engaged the participants was to bring them close to the threshold of the unknown, a place where they had no anticipated answers and did not have well-grooved habits for how to react. I found that space of the unknown both comfortable and threatening (*a paradoxical sensation I felt beneath the stillness I thought was necessary to belong*). I could feel the inviting potential that was beneath the threat that ambiguity posed, where potential and a place for deep learning dwelt. What I also found was that very few of the participants had the same level of enthusiasm as I did for the vital learning through the unknown that an experience of ambiguity brings. I designed learning experiences to help mitigate the fallacy of knowing as the only source of problem-solving. I soon found that, for most, learning meant learning the right answer. And it turns out, for most, far too much adult learning is geared toward that aim—to save you from the dangers of the unknown. The programs I designed fostered courage and bravery in the face of the unknown. They were also confrontational spaces where there was more effort spent on finding ways to avoid learning how to learn from the not fore-known. I was 30 years old when I realized I had exhausted my knowledge and tolerance for frustration, facilitating learning through the unknown, and, ironically, turned to further knowledge acquisition as a remedy, in the form of doctoral education. I was then stuck in a polarity—knowing that can lead to liberation, and knowing that is reliable in solving problems—vacillating between both of these poles I did not create new futures.

For my dissertation, I turned to complexity science, quantum theory, constructive developmental theory, evolutionary biology, pragmatism, Buddhism, and mystical teachings to help me understand the vital forces of the unknown by seeking others' lived experiences of ambiguity through in-depth phenomenological interviews (Nicolaides, 2008). As I walked more surely into ambiguity, alone and with those who would come with me as part of my dissertation research, I experienced and identified many of the enfolding gifts of ambiguity. In particular, I found that when a person holds a more complex way of knowing, they are open to befriending ambiguity. I discovered that when one displayed a greater comfort with ambiguity and a greater ability to re-order the sensations that ambiguity stirs in creative ways, ambiguity was not so threatening. I began my academic career with the gifts of my research in the form of orienting principles for learning through ambiguity. In my early research, I described this process of knowing as learning through complexity.

This brings me to the present. Another decade has passed, and in spite of a decade more of playing with ambiguity, dressing it in costumes that appear easier to encounter than its own raw force, I find that I am disillusioned by the lack of potency that most adult learning programs generate. Learning as a way of seeking knowledge is still "business-as-usual" for the most part in classrooms, training centers, and institutions of higher education. Findings from my research began to shape an idea that the unknown, the territory where ambiguity lives, has a potency that can become generative (Nicolaides, 2008, 2015; Nicolaides & Lim, 2020). By *generative* I mean ways of actualizing potential creatively in multiple ways. I began small experiments with my doctoral students and in my advanced seminars to fold generativity into the already-existing adult education paradigm that governs most of the adult learning today. These small experiments have led to fissures, *Ruptures* of insight, and moments of generativity for my students and myself. However, I have come to accept that I am still trapped in between worlds of what is expected, recognized, and sought after as "learning" and the potential that lies beneath the unknown when we let what cannot be fore-known into the territory of our inquiry.

How do we build a just and equitable society to which all of us can belong? How does adult learning make personal and societal belonging real? These are the deep inquiries that I have been following for a long time. Answers to such inquiries are never coming; they are always in a state of becoming. This state of learning from the not fore-known I describe as *generative knowing*: ways of being and becoming activating potential creatively. Adult learning has its roots in the potential of liberation, yet it also remains trapped in a paradigm that perpetuates structures where learning contributes to maintaining injustice and inequality. I am curious to uncover how adult learning can make society more spacious and open for all beings and how learning can grow capacities in beings that allow for a more inclusive society. This is the big inquiry that has brought me to my vocation as an adult educator. This book uncovers what I have encountered as I live and walk alongside this inquiry. Potential is always present; this I have learned from quantum theory (Barad, 2007) and the essential meaning of complexity—multiplicity and interconnection (Nicolaides & Yorks, 2008). Generative knowing activates "a door in every moment" (Nicolaides, 2008) when we accompany inquiry in ways that bring forth a multiplicity of ways of being and becoming. This entanglement may seem odd, but it feels ripe to me. The irony is that potential is always ready to be activated and yet cannot be fore-known. Inquiring beneath the territory of experience, the unknown side of inquiry, learning becomes generative, opening up ways of being and becoming.

An Inquiry into Potential Becoming Generative

I have had this book in me for a long time, in that part of me that has been waiting for me to find the courage to write it. I applied for academic research leave in 2019 to dedicate the first part of 2020 to writing a book I have been imagining since I completed my doctoral dissertation in 2008. The fall semester before my research leave, I took a step in the direction of writing by working with a writing coach who helped me to design a structure for my book. A different experience crystalized that the writing would work with the *stuff* (data) of the truth of my own lived and living experience to convey the mystery of generative knowing with freedom, the subject of Chapter 4 herein. Generative knowing is a resonance, a sensation of grace given, a gift received, and an offering. This book will illuminate generative knowing as

Prologue

ways of being and becoming, actualizing potential creatively by poking fissures of light in the territory beneath living experience.

The book is guided by inquiry that I am still living. How can adult learning make new worlds for self and society real? To move beneath this inquiry demands many departures from the known territories of adult learning. Interestingly, as I write this book, UNESCO has published its new future for education vision and aim. In it, the vision is described as *Futures of Education: Learning to Become* [italics in original]. This initiative is "intended to catalyze a global debate on how knowledge and learning can shape the future of humanity and the planet" (UNESCO, 2021). I find this invitation resonating with the content of this book, activating new lines of inquiry and conversation about how learning to become is the future of education.

This book is a reading that provokes a move from an observer of distant mental categories to a participant of lived realities. The vulnerability of this text provides openings—spaces—to receive the structures that always live beneath us, not yet seen (Gebser, 1977; cited in Johnson, 2019). To go beneath experience, where learning is becoming, requires a co-operation with the reader in that what I write should stir something in you (Dewey, 1934). The possibility that this book offers is a resonance with something that is all-ready, present, and received (Johnson, 2019). Generative knowing is not the content of learning; it is a process of not seeking fore-knowing (Deleuze & Guattari, 1987). It is what Gebser (1997) describes as *"Awaring"* (Gebser, 1997). *Awaring* makes visible the openings and expanse of the whole of experience, capable of overcoming fragmentation and creatively breaking forth new worlds (Pendleton-Julian & Brown, 2018). I borrow from Gebser's (1997) phenomenology of consciousness and cultural philosophy the language of *Awaring* to denote freedom. *Awaring* is the activation of awakening. To become aware (awareness, awakening) is a mental activity that divides the process of generative knowing. To signal the freedom, more rhizomatic entanglement, that generative knowing is, I use the language of *Awaring* to denote that actualizing of potential, a freedom *from* and *for* the boundless world (Johnson, 2019).

I invite you to read this book as an intentional practice: that as a reader, you continue to observe your own experience of reading and the sensations that arise through this process, as if you were holding the cultural "artifacts" that are about to be described in your own hands or, at the very least, in your own mind's eye. Welcome any sudden receptivity, any inward stirrings, and moments of felt-sense, no matter how small the feelings and no matter how often these stirrings might wish to return you to the world as you know it (Johnson, 2019). *Felt-sense* is a philosophical concept described by Gendlin (1978) from physics and biology, to understand the human body differently. Your body is not a machine, but rather an intricate interaction with everything around you, which is why it "knows" so much just in being. Your ongoing living makes new evolution and history happen—now. You can sense your living body directly under your thoughts and memories and under your familiar feelings. The self-sense happens at a deeper level than your feelings. Under them, you can discover a physically sensed "murky zone" that you can enter and open. This is the source from which new responses emerge. Once found, this felt-sense is a palpable presence underneath. Watch for those stirrings as a practice while reading this book. The book is fluid, moving beneath the past, present, and emerging future (Nicolaides & Marsick, 2015). Moving between known theory and new nomadic theoretical tones that express ontology as it becomes many epistemologies, making ethical action more comfortable (Mälkki, 2020).

    The book begins by presenting a nomadic theory of adult learning, generative learning, followed by a discussion of the theoretical lineages from which generative learning evolves. The first three chapters frame the theoretical and methodological ground from which generative knowing emerges. A presentation of the phenomenological approach I take in following the phenomenon is the subject of Chapter 3. The chapters that follow uncover three different rich narratives of lived experience that tell the story of generativity as it emerges in the relatedness of the storyteller and me. Chapter 4 features my own story, Chapter 5 in relationship with my mother's experience of the Six-Day War, and Chapter 6 in relationship with my father's narrative about his early life in Palestine and the displacement he experienced (and that I, too, carry as a lineage holder of my family's trauma. In Chapter 7 Ahreum Lim, a doctoral candidate, applies generative knowing to her own experience with learning for a future of work. The final chapter tells a new story of learning that is free to create and respond to an evolving boundless world. The book unfolds in an incongruent time sequence, meaning that the narrative arc of these stories travels across lifetimes, ancestral histories, and geographical locations. Such is the life of a nomad.

References

Barad, K. (2007). *Meeting the universe halfway: Quantum physics and the entanglement of matter and meaning.* Duke University Press.
Deleuze, G., & Guattari, F. (1987). *A thousand plateaus: Capitalism and schizophrenia* (B. Massumi, Trans.). University of Minnesota Press. (Original work published 1980)
Deleuze, G., & Guattari, F. (1994). *What is philosophy?* (H. Tomlinson, & G. Burchell, Trans.). Columbia University Press. (Original work published 1991)
Dewey, J. (1934). *Art as experience.* Penguin.
Gebser, J. (1997). *The ever-present origin* (N. Barstad & A. Mickunas, Trans.). Ohio University Press. (Original work published 1987)
Gendlin, E. T. (1978). *Focusing.* Everest House.
Johnson, J. (2019). *Seeing through the world: Jean Gebser and integral consciousness.* Revelore Press.
Mälkki, K. (2020). *Spaces of care and multiple voices.* SAGE Publications.
Nicolaides, A., & Yorks, L. (2008). An epistemology of learning through. *Emergence: Complexity & Organization, 10*(1).
Nicolaides, A. (2015). Generative learning: Adults learning within ambiguity. *Adult Education Quarterly, 65*(3), 179–195.
Nicolaides, A., & Lim, A. (2020). Undergoing the experiences of the COVID-19 pandemic as ruptures in American civil society create conditions for right action. *Reflective Practice, 21*(6), 844–860. https://doi.org/10.1080/14623943.2020.1821632
Nicolaides, A., & Marsick, V. J. (2016). Understanding adult learning in the midst of complex social "liquid modernity." *New Directions for Adult and Continuing Education, 2016*(149), 9–20.
Pendleton-Jullian, A., & Brown, J. S. (2018). *Design unbound: Designing for emergence in a white water world, Volume 2: Ecologies of change.* MIT Press.
UNESCO. (2021). *UNESCO futures of education: Learning to become.* https://en.unesco.org/futuresofeducation/initiative

ONE

 Generative Knowing: A Nomadic
Theory of Adult Learning

Everything Begins Beneath

UNCOVERING THE TERRITORY BENEATH THE experience of experience is a domain of adult learning that is underexplored. I am writing this book as an exploration of deep learning, not evident on the surface of experience, but rather, the landscape of what John O'Donohue (Irish poet and philosopher) described as "the invisible world" that is constantly intertwining with what we can know and see. This invisible world requires a slowing down and softening toward, in order to experience the sensations that experience reveals. It is to this invisible world that my research turned, in order to uncover the potential that lies in a world not fore-known. Through my research on how adults learn and make meaning, especially in the face of the unknown, I have come into contact with a vast territory from which a generative way of learning emerges. I conducted a phenomenological study from 2006 to 2008, in which I sought to follow the phenomenon of learning-from-ambiguity. In that study I defined *ambiguity* as an encounter with an appearance of reality that is at first unrecognizable, oblique, simultaneously evoking fear of "no-cognition" and the potential for hope for multiple meanings irresolvable by reference to context alone (Nicolaides, 2015). As my research has evolved, so has my understanding of ambiguity as a territory of the unknown that cannot be fore-known and that evokes a quest for certainty—a fool's errand, as John Dewey declared (1934). From this inquiry, I discovered that when conditions such as one's way of knowing allow a close encounter with the ambiguity that complexity brings, learning emerges. The learning that emerges invites the sensations of ambiguity to re-order how knowing becomes known. It is paradoxical that learning has its own side, so to speak, to treat learning as more than that which we seek to know and instead explore learning as an intra-active exchange (human-more-than-human-ambiguity) that reveals potential from the not fore-known. I seek to remain in the ironic combination of the quest for certainty and the potential received from the unknown. That is where my inquiry remains, and from this ground emerges learning that is generative in ways of knowing where being and becoming catalyze potential.

I define *generative knowing* as ways of being and becoming that activate potential creatively. *Becoming* denotes the slow turn toward and softening toward the sensations of experience as we undergo, or go beneath, encounters with the not-foreknown. The invisible world of the unknown is a territory that pulls on my curiosity and has guided a long arc of inquiry that has become my research as a scholar of adult learning. Becoming describes the rhythm of learning that I describe as part of generative knowing. Becoming generates new awareness coming from the invisible world where learning emerges from the entangled intra-active aspects of our identities with the many forces that contexts include (human-more-than-human-ambiguity). Becoming troubles the notion that learning is only human-centered. Becoming signals that learning is intra-active in that learning exists in the intra-action of identities, systems, and human and more-than-human relationships that our social and natural contexts contain. Becoming is a concept, a problem that unfolds many perspectives, nuances, and senses. For Deleuze and Guattari (1980/1987), becoming anticipates beyond knowing, control, and our desire to consume and possess. Becoming extends beyond the knowable and logic, toward sensing, experimentation, and risk. *Generative* signifies the entangled emergence of insight, trustworthy to guide ethical action(s) that are already intra-active with all matterings (Barad, 2007). *Matterings* is a concept taken from quantum physics that tells us that the void (the unknowable) is an endless exploration of all possible couplings of virtual particles, a "scene of wild activities" (Barad, 2015, p. 393–396). What holds special meaning in terms of adult learning is the notion of the void where matter (as small as electrons and as vast as a tropical forest) is already in dynamic play, intra-acting. This territory, where matter is always in intra-active play, lies beneath the territory of experience, where everything is already open and not yet a response.

Departing from the rich epistemology of adult learning theories that have influenced my thinking for the past 20 years, I want to uncover the generative aspects of learning as a force that creates different ways of knowing, making the intra-active play that intertwines self and society visible and vital. Generative knowing has emerged from the margins. It is a nomadic concept, fluid and in motion across many territories of experience. As an inquiry, generative knowing acts nomadically in that what it reveals rises from beneath the invisible world where the stuff of self and society are deeply entangled. In this chapter, I name generative knowing: ways of being and becoming that creatively liberate potential; as a nomadic theory of learning that will be exposed through the chapters that follow.

Honoring The Lineage of Adult Learning and Evolving

Learning signifies processes by which what is knowable becomes known through experience. Dewey (1934) defines learning in terms of experience, reflection, continuity, and interactivity. When learning happens, it eventually solidifies into reliable truths that become a shortcut for taking action or making decisions—a habit of learning is formed and becomes rigid (Mezirow, 1991). Learning has at times been appropriated as one of the strategies by which human beings remain in control of their reality (Siemens, 2007). Remaining in control is a dominant approach to learning how to learn that governs the many processes of learning that have been codified and reproduced (Brookfield, 1994; Elias & Merriam, 1995). Learning approaches based on the philosophies of humanism, constructivism, and pragmatism theorize about produced multiple ways of knowing—intellectual, volitional, emotional, sensory, imaginal, aesthetic, and transformative—each with methods aimed to free agency and solve problems which, at the same time, reproduce learning outcomes that preserve a form of control and self-protection (Brookfield, 1986; Jarvis, 1992; Kegan, 1982). Many adult learning approaches make way for learning to take place on behalf of individual agency (i.e., transformative learning), organizational goals (i.e., social network learning), and sometimes societal transformation (i.e., social movement learning in the form of the Civil Rights Movement of the 1960s; HIV ACT UP in New York, 1987–1993; and the catalyst of Black Lives Matter in the summer of 2020). There is a need to explore and renew the philosophical underpinnings of adult learning, as persistent inequality, social fragmentation, and political extremism are bringing many societies to a point of crisis (Eshenbacher & Fleming, 2020; Finnegan, 2019; Nicolaides & Lim, 2020). Advances in digital communication, artificial intelligence, and biotechnology have great potential, but they also raise serious ethical and governance concerns, especially as promises of innovation and technological change have an uneven record of contributing to human flourishing (Lim & Nicolaides, under review). These new and persistent forces overwhelm and intersect with processes of learning, challenging conventional knowledge and adult learning. What if adult learning were a way for creating conditions to pose different inquiries and invent alternative forms of agency that shaped a future where learning as a process of becoming was a lifelong endeavor of creative inquiry within the complexity of an ever-evolving diversity (UNESCO, 2021)?

Generative knowing begins beneath the experience of experience, where the sensations of already-intra-active dynamics of self and society are entangled. Beneath the experience of experience is an invisible world that is vibrant, with root systems that are moving deeper into and across the compost of experiences, making branches that reach out toward sunlight always in a state of sensing and becoming (Deleuze & Guattari, 1980/1987). Generative knowing is akin to the process of cultivating the capacity to see through structures of knowing that have become expectations (Gebser, 1997; cited in Johnson, 2019). Generative knowing is akin to stumbling in the dark, a risk one takes when walking in the dark, trusting that you will find your way. Polanyi (1966) describes this as the tacit dimension of knowing, a structure of knowledge from which responsible human action emerges in a lucid instant. *Undergoing experience* is a phrase describing the descent into the experience in order to have it, to become intertwined with the already-there potentials that consciousness brings into beingness. These gifts of potential are a living mystery waiting to be received from beneath the experience. Undergoing experience is the process of generative knowing that Dewey (1934) and James (1907) felt in the folds between discipline and passion, which gave rise to American Pragmatism. Undergoing experience is the wisdom of the sociocultural intuition of Vygotsky (1934) that there is a place from where something new comes, just beyond what we wish to control to know and what may be revealed in the interaction between all things that matter in our self, social, and cultural milieu. Experience, and what emerges from its own side to guide ethical human action, is what the humanist's desire for freedom aspires to (Knowles, 1977; Lindeman, 1926). Activating potential is embedded in the radical activism of Freire (1970), in which learning is a force of good for all people, regardless of social class, race, gender, or ethnicity (Freire & Horton, 1990). Learning as ways of knowing is how the constructivists map, across an unfolding life course, the potential that learning may expose (Gilligan, 2003; Kegan, 1982,

1998; Kohlberg, 1994; Perry, 1999). At the heart of transformative learning is the promise to catalyze a re-ordering of perspective so that more knowing can be recognized (Mezirow, 1991, 2000, 2003).

Understanding the experience of experience is what the cognitivist scientist yearns to measure and set to warp speed (Siemens, 2015; Wittrock, 1974). Upending learning is how the postmodernists see and articulate in more than words that experience comes first and, much later, recognition and knowable knowing (Heron, 1996; Jarvis, 1992). Undergoing as a movement is what critical theorists feel deeply and grieve (Bauman, 2006; Brookfield, 2004; Rorty, 2000). Feminists have known all along that knowing does not come in one form; they have been silenced only to be heard anew (Ahmed, 2017; Butler, 2006; hooks, 2003; Lorde, 2020). This mystery is already felt by the Indigenous knowledges that were forced to hide and/or be left behind to lay in wait until regenerated in a time of pause and pain that civil unrest and a global pandemic have ignited (Kimmerer, 2020).

Adult learning as we know it has been defined, redefined, played with like Silly Putty made into so many different shapes, to keep its potential (Braidotti, 2011) in a state of control . . . to keep the science and hide the mystery. As a dynamic living polarity, science and mystery are deeply intertwined beneath experience (Dewey, 1934; Nicolaides & Lim, 2020). Science is useful for the kind of inquiry that seeks verifiable answers. Mystery is a guide for inquiry that begins beneath experience, in the compost of the experiences where sensations rise up into consciousness (Heron, 1992). Science has its place in forms of understanding that preserve and protect (Elias & Merriam, 1995). Mystery reveals and gives meaning to the interconnectedness of all matter, making things anew. Both are true, meaning both are valid portals into making sense of the experiences that forge futures that are never fully knowable until they are revealed and received (Scharmer, 2019).

Getting Adult Learning into Good Trouble

Getting adult learning into "good trouble" (John Lewis, may he rest in power) is what I do when I reveal generative knowing as a nomadic theory of adult learning. To accomplish this unveiling, I engage in the process of diffractive analysis (Barad, 2014; Mazzei, 2014; Nicolaides & Scully-Russ, 2018) of theoretically established concepts (as I did in the previous section, thinking with the different perspectives that make the field of adult learning) that influence the emergence of generative knowing. These theoretical concepts are derived from the epistemology of adult learning as undergoing experience, as described by Dewey and Follet (Dewey, 1934; Fenwick, 2000; Follet, 1924), generative learning from the perspective of the cognitive sciences (Wittrock, 1974), and triple-loop learning (Torbert et al., 1972; Torbert, 2004). Diffraction is a dynamism, not an event, that is integral to the continuous repatterning of a field. As the field unfolds, it also enfolds upon itself in unpredictable ways that imbue each moment with infinite possibilities. In this process, I dance with this form of diffractive analysis to explore and precipitate a repatterning of my understanding of adult learning, with implications for revealing a theory of adult learning that rises from the margins. Following the advice of Mazzei (2014), I use diffractive analysis to plug in ideas, fragments, concepts, sensations, selves, and perspectives as I read the concepts and theories through one another. My aim is to give rise to unpredictable and productive thoughts and meanings and to take this analysis in new and continuously enfolding directions and forms. This approach demands that we affirm all the theories available, rather than oppose or critique them, because they matter for the many ways that I understand and envision (Benavente, 2010) the context and processes of adult learning today.

Nomadic Theory

I present generative knowing as a nomadic theory of adult learning. I borrow the concept of a nomadic theory from Braidotti (2019), whose affirmative ethics have influenced my thinking about the "stuff" of generative knowing.

> Nomadic theory moves beyond the categories of self-reflexive-individualism and linear progressivism and rests on a process ontology that challenges the traditional equation of subjectivity with rational consciousness, resisting the reduction of both to a linear vision of progress . . . . Instead of deference to the authority of the past, nomad thought proposes the fleeting copresence of multiple time zones, in a time continuum that activates and "deterritorialized stable identities . . . ." Nomadic implies a double commitment, on the one hand, to processes of change, and on the other, to a strong ethics of the ecosophical sense of community—of "our" being this together. (Braidotti, 2011, pp. 209–211)

As I have worked to describe generative knowing, it has been helpful to conceptualize it as a nomadic theory of adult learning extending and claiming Follett's (1924) intuition that adult learning is always in an intra-active process of becoming.

To bring about this concept-creation, generative knowing, I engaged in what Deleuze describes as nomadic thinking (Deleuze, 1994) and put into service the method of affirmative ethics (Braidotti, 2011) to trouble adult learning and to explore not-foreknowing. *Becoming nomadic* marks the process of affirmative transformation of pain and loss into the active production of multiple forms of belonging and complex allegiances that are the stuff of generative knowing (Braidotti, 2011; Deleuze, 1994). The metaphor of the nomad is potent, indicating a dynamic and evolving character of philosophical concepts that do not have forever-fixed and eternal meanings independent of context, time, place, subject, or culture. Nomads are excluded from history, yet they break through into history by virtue of their very geography, that is, a movement that cannot be controlled.

Generative knowing as a nomadic theory functions at different speeds, moves on different timelines, and is fueled by radically different ethical effects. It departs from the flat territories of conventional theories of adult learning occupied mostly by the humanist, constructivist, and pragmatist views. I invoke nomadic thinking (Deleuze & Guattari, 1987) to signal movement from the ontology of experience, because generative knowing is recording both what we experience/are ceasing to be—the "no longer"—and what we experience/are in the process of becoming—the "not-yet." *Not-yet* is a metaphor used by educational philosopher Maxine Greene (1998) in describing the processes of becoming "real"—recognition of patterns of difference becoming resonance that makes for a life of learning (Bateson, 1991).

Learning That Is Fluid

Thinking is about acknowledging, capturing, and working with extensive and intensive ethical relationality. This book argues that thinking with and through experience within complex temporalities (Alhadeff-Jones, 2021) involves the creation of new concepts and adequate figurations, to express them ethically, for this contemporary moment in the evolution of a field committed to the just unfolding of self and society. The main criteria I will use are non-linearity and the powers of memory and the imagination, as a strategy of defamiliarization (Braidotti, 2013). Generative knowing is always not-yet and becoming. Generative knowing is a way to strike a balance in "temporal as well as spatial terms between the 'no-longer' and the 'not yet'" (Braidotti, 2019, p. 68). This requires finding some synchronicity between complex and multiple foldings, and different flows of time sequences. That is to say: generative knowing resonates with the multiple ways in which humanity with all intra-actions is currently being recomposed.

Adult education as a field of practice is grappling presently with how adults learn in a world being recomposed by a global pandemic and the *Ruptures* that have emerged from its influence. The work of Thomas and Brown (2011) explores the need for a new learning theory that can keep up with the rapid rate of change. Thomas and Brown see a shift in learning from *learning about* to *learning to be* to *learning to become*. Generative knowing is a nomadic theory of learning to become (Nicolaides, 2015; Nicolaides & Lim, 2020), articulating different ways of learning and the capacities that such knowing demands for "radical innovation and rapid transformation in the face of continuous disruption" (Melacarne & Nicolaides, 2019, p. 23).

Aspects of Generative Knowing

I grappled with how to describe facets of generative knowing in a way that captures the processual dynamics of learning as undergoing experience. I settled on using the term "aspects" to connote the rhythms of generative knowing in motion. I will describe three aspects of generative knowing: *Ruptures*, *In-scending*, and *Awaring*. The role of connected imagination is one way to grasp generative knowing as an emerging ontology of adult learning. I borrow philosophically from Polanyi's (1966) musings on the tacit dimension of learning, where learning is a way to encounter the unknown. Encountering the unknown takes practice and intentional paying of attention that you cannot leave behind. Not leaving the intention behind demands imagination to see in the dark. Seeing in the dark catalyzes *Ruptures* in knowledge. Intentionally encountering the experience of the unknown *Ruptures* knowing. This is where generative knowing begins, with the *Ruptures* that do not leave being and becoming behind, meaning that the ontology of the experience leads the way while the epistemology of the experience shifts into the background for a new way of knowing to emerge. Engaging the *Ruptures* is demanding; courageous vulnerability accompanies listening into the luminous darkness of the invisible world of experience. To listen into the dark requires that we *In-scend* beneath the experience into the territory of the not fore-known. *In-scend* is a word of my own making. It is the intentional movement of inquiry that follows the sensations of the experience in order to undergo it, to listen from the inside of the at-first darkness that is the side beneath (as Dewey describes it, undergoing) experience. This aspect of generative knowing, to *In-scend*, is a practice of inquiry into the ontology of experience. Ambiguity is the currency of this practice in that the inquiry moves in spaces of entanglement with past, present, and future that the ontology of experience does not try to resolve. This fluid timelessness allows the practice of *In-scending* to inquire into the compost of experience where potential is all-ready, not-yet activated. That activation demands another practice: the practice of placing a different kind of attention on the sensations of the experience of *In-scending*, following which the sensations awaken resonances that in time emerge as moral codes for ethical response. This different kind of attention I describe as *Awaring*, the active opening to potential. *Awaring* is a concept that I borrow from Gebser's (in Johnson, 2019) phenomenology of consciousness and cultural philosophy. *Awaring* denotes a liberational quality, the overcoming of the "mere antithesis of affirmation and negation" (Gebser, 1997; cited in Johnson, 2019). In Gebser's work, the prefix "a" stands for freedom in all its qualities of manifestation (*a*rational, *a*perspectival, *a*mensional), a freedom *from* and *for* the boundless world (Johnson, 2019). *Awaring* describes the freedom to activate potential creatively, which inspires the action of generative knowing as ways of being and becoming. *Awaring* is the capacity of seeing in the dark that does not seek first to know; instead, *Awaring* is the culmination of generative knowing, in that potential is activated in a multiplicity of ways of being and becoming that give flight to response-able actions. *Awaring* is the process of naming and freeing potential, giving potential the power to become a force for action. Generative knowing is a nomadic theory that allows for learning that responds to experience as it is happening, giving rise to essential possibilities. Generative knowing activates potential in ways of being and becoming that denotes joyous inquiry, intensive experimentation with the unknown, expressed as difference in and of itself, and giving rise to something new. This book is such a becoming, making my experience something new.

References

Ahmed, A. (2017). *Living a feminist life*. Duke University Press.
Alhadeff-Jones, M. (2021). Learning from the whirlpools of existence: Crises and transformative processes as complex and rhythmic phenomena. *European Journal for Research on the Education and Learning of Adults, 12*(3), 311–326.
Barad, K. (2007). *Meeting the universe halfway: Quantum physics and the entanglement of matter and meaning*. Duke University Press.
Barad, K. (2014). Diffracting diffraction: Cutting together-apart. *Parallax, 20*(3), 168–187. https://doi.org/10.1080/13534645.2014.927623
Barad, K. (2015). Transmaterialities: Trans*/matter/realities and queer political imaginings. *GLQ: A Journal of Lesbian and Gay Studies, 21*(2–3), 387–422.
Bateson, G. (1991). *A sacred unity: Further steps to an ecology of mind*. Harper San Francisco.
Bauman, Z. (2006). *Liquid fear* (1st ed.). Wiley.
Benavente, B. R. (2010). Re(con)figuring the ethico-onto-epistemological questions of matter. *Graduate Journal of Social Science, 7*(1), 83–86.
Braidotti, R. (2011). *Nomadic theory: The portable Rosi Braidotti*. Columbia University Press.
Braidotti, R. (2013). *The posthuman*. Polity Press.
Braidotti, R. (2019). *Posthuman knowledge*. Wiley.
Brookfield, S. (1986). *Understanding and facilitating adult learning: A comprehensive analysis of principles and effective practices*. Open University Press.
Brookfield, S. (1994). Tales from the dark side: A phenomenography of adult critical reflection. *International Journal of Lifelong Education, 13*(3), 203–216. https://doi.org/10.1080/0260137940130303
Brookfield, S. (2004). *The power of critical theory: Liberating adult learning and teaching*. Wiley.
Butler, J. (2006). *Gender trouble: Feminism and the subversion of identity*. Routledge.
Deleuze, G. (1986). *Kafka: Toward a minor literature*. University of Minnesota Press.
Deleuze, G. (1994). *Difference and repetition*. Columbia University Press.
Deleuze, G., & Guattari, F. (1987). *A thousand plateaus: Capitalism and schizophrenia* (B. Massumi, Trans.). University of Minnesota Press. (Original work published 1980)
Dewey, J. (1934). *Art as experience*. Penguin.
Dewey, J. (1966). Democracy and education (1916). In J. A. Boydston (Ed.). *The Middle Works of John Dewey, 9, 1899–1924*. Southern Illinois University Press.
Elias, J. L., & Merriam, S. B. (1995). *Philosophical foundations of adult education*. Krieger Publishing Company.
Eschenbacher, S., & Fleming, T. (2020). Transformative dimensions of lifelong learning: Mezirow, Rorty and COVID-19. *International Review of Education, 66*(5), 657–672. https://doi.org/10.1007/s11159-020-09859-6
Fenwick, T. J. (2000). Expanding conceptions of experiential learning: A review of the five contemporary perspectives on cognition. *Adult Education Quarterly, 50*(4), 243–272. https://doi.org/10.1177/07417130022087035
Finnegan, F. (2019). "Freedom is a very fine thing": Individual and collective forms of emancipation in transformative learning. In A. Kokkos, F. Finnegan, & T. Fleming (Eds.), *European

perspectives on transformation theory (pp. 43–57). Springer. https://doi.org/10.1007/978-3-030-19159-7_4

Follett, M. P. (1924). *Creative experience*. Longmans, Green and Company.

Freire, P. (1970). *Pedagogy of the oppressed*. Herder and Herder.

Freire, P., & Horton, M. (1990). *We make the road by walking: Conversations on education and social change*. Temple University Press.

Gilligan, C. (2003). *In a different voice: Psychological theory and women's development*. Harvard University Press.

Greene, M. (1998). Moral and Political Perspectives: The Tensions of Choice. *Educational Researcher, 27*(9), 18–20. https://doi.org/10.3102/0013189X027009018

Heron, J. (1992). *Feeling and personhood: Psychology in another key*. Sage.

Heron, J. (1996). *Co-operative inquiry: Research into the human condition*. Sage.

hooks, b. (2003). *Teaching community: A pedagogy of hope*. Psychology Press.

International Commission on the Futures of Education (2021). *Reimagining our futures together: a new social contract for education*. UNESCO. https://unesdoc.unesco.org/ark:/48223/pf0000379707.locale=en

James, W. (1907). *Pragmatism, a new name for some old ways of thinking: Popular lectures on philosophy*. Longmans, Green.

Jarvis, P. (1992). *Paradoxes of Learning: On becoming an individual in Society*. Wiley.

Johnson, J. (2019). *Seeing through the world: Jean Gebser and integral consciousness*. Revelore Press.

Kegan, R. (1982). *The evolving self: Problem and process in human development*. Harvard University Press.

Kegan, R. (1998). *In over our heads: The mental demands of modern life*. Harvard University Press.

Kimmerer, R. W. (2020). *Braiding sweetgrass: Indigenous wisdom, scientific knowledge and the teachings of plants*. Penguin Books.

Knowles, M. (1977). Adult learning processes: Pedagogy and andragogy. *Religious Education, 72*(2), 202–211. https://doi.org/10.1080/0034408770720210

Kohlberg, L. (1994). *Moral development: Kohlberg's original study of moral development (No. 3)*. Taylor & Francis.

Lindeman, E. (1926). *The meaning of adult education*. New Republic, Inc.

Lorde, A. (2020). *The cancer journals*. Penguin.

Mazzei, L. A. (2014). Beyond an easy sense: A diffractive analysis. *Qualitative Inquiry, 20*(6), 742–746. https://doi.org/10.1177/1077800414530257

Melacarne, C., & Nicolaides, A. (2019). Developing professional capability: Growing capacity and competencies to meet complex workplace demands. *New Directions for Adult and Continuing Education* (163), 37–51. https://doi.org/10.1002/ace.20340

Mezirow, J. (1991). *Transformative dimensions of adult learning*. ERIC.

Mezirow, J. (2000). *Learning as transformation: Critical perspectives on a theory in progress*. United Kingdom: Wiley.

Mezirow, J. (2003). Transformative learning as discourse. *Journal of Transformative Education, 1*(1), 58–63. https://doi.org/10.1177/1541344603252172

Nicolaides, A. (2008). *Learning their way through ambiguity: Explorations of how nine developmentally mature adults make sense of ambiguity.* EdD dissertation, Teachers College, Columbia University.

Nicolaides, A. (2015). Generative learning: Adults learning within ambiguity. *Adult Education Quarterly, 65*(3), 179–195.

Nicolaides, A., & Lim, A. (2020). Undergoing the experiences of the COVID-19 pandemic as ruptures in American civil society create conditions for right action. *Reflective Practice, 21*(6), 844–860.

Nicolaides, A., & Scully-Russ, E. (2018). Connections, questions, controversies, and the potential paths forward. *New Directions for Adult and Continuing Education, 2018*(159), 103-124. https://doi.org/10.1002/ace.20290

Nicolaides, A., & Yorks, L. (2008). An epistemology of learning through. *Emergence: Complexity & Organization, 10*(1): 50–61.

Perry, Jr., W. G. (1999). *Forms of intellectual and ethical development in the college years: A scheme.* Jossey-Bass.

Polanyi, M. (1966). *The tacit dimension.* Doubleday.

Rorty, R. (2000). Pragmatism. *International Journal of Psycho-Analysis, 81*(4), 819–823.

Scharmer, C. O. (2019). *Essentials der theorie U: Grundprinzipien und anwendungen.* Carl-Auer Verlag.

Siemens, G. (2007). Connectivism: Creating a learning ecology in distributed environments. In T. Hug (Ed.), *Didactics of microlearning: Concepts, discourses and examples* (pp. 53–68). Waxmann Verlag.

Siemens, G. (2015). *Preparing for the digital university: A review of the history and current state of distance, blended, and online learning.* Link Research Lab. http://linkresearchlab.org/PreparingDigitalUniversity.pdf

Thomas, D., & Brown, J. S. (2011). *A new culture of learning: Cultivating the imagination for a world of constant change.* CreateSpace, Lexington, KY.

Torbert, W. R. (2004). *Action inquiry: The secret of timely and transforming leadership.* Berrett-Koehler Publishers.

Torbert, W. R., Glueck, E., & Elmering, H. (1972). *Learning from experience: Toward consciousness.* Columbia University Press.

Vygotsky, L. S. (1934). *Thought and language.* MIT Press.

Wittrock, M. C. (1974). Learning as a generative process. *Educational Psychologist, 11*(2), 87–95. https://doi.org/10.1080/00461527409529129

Yorks, L., & Nicolaides, A. (2013). Toward an integral approach for evolving mindsets for generative learning and timely action in the midst of ambiguity. *Teachers College Record, 115*(8), 1–26.

TWO

 A Brief Review of Adult Learning Theory

Adult Learning Foundations

BREAKING WITH THE CONVENTIONAL LANGUAGE of adult education (mostly pragmatism, humanism, and constructivism) makes way for new thinking from different philosophical foundations that have accompanied me as I inquire into the not-foreknown—a territory for learning that arises from the sensations beneath experience (Nicolaides, 2008, 2015). All adult learning, regardless of history and epistemology, involves the intra-penetration (Dewey, 1934; Torbert et al., 1972) of experience that invites processes of intra-active (Barad, 2007) meaning-making (being and becoming) that shape action, including inaction. Generative connotes relational entanglements that are beneath experience and already intra-active with all that matters, including self and society (Barad, 2003; Braidotti, 2019; Maturana & Varela, 1987; Scharmer, 2018). In 1924, Mary Parker Follett (1868–1933), described that the keys to creativity, will, and power lie in deep experiencing. Like Dewey's "undergoing," surrendering the totality of one's self to each new experience, Follett states:

> All that I am, all that life has made me, every past experience that I have had— woven into the tissue of my life—I must give to the new experience....

We integrate our experience, and then the richer human being that we are goes into the new experience; again we give our self and always by giving rise above the old self. (1924, pp. 136–137)

True to her Gestalt influence, Follett saw everything in relation. She described how we co-create one another in relationship by circular response. Through circular response intra-actions we create each other. In this co-creation, Follett describes how we can meet together in experience to evoke learning and development in one another.... The essence of experience, the law of relation, is reciprocal freeing: here is the "rock" and the substance of the human spirit. (Alhadeff-Jones, 2021)

She continues to describe this relationality as the truth of intra-action: evocation.

We are all rooted in that great unknown in which are the infinite latents of becoming. And these latents are evoked, called forth into visibility, summoned, by the action and reaction of one on the other. All [human and more-than-human] interaction should be the evocation by each from the other of new forms undreamed of before, and all interchanges that is not evocation should be eschewed. Release, evocation—evocation by release, release by evocation—this is the fundamental law of the universe. To free the energies of the human spirit is the high potentiality of all human association. (Follett, 1924, p. 76)

Follett connects directly to Dewey's concept of undergoing as a distinguishing feature of learning from experience. Learning is not something that is guaranteed. Dewey was clear in his deliberations about learning and society that they are intimate partners not guaranteed to *penetrate* each other. Only when we undergo and have an experience are we penetrated; then, we learn and act in accord, so as to create something new that changes everything that matters (d'Agnese, 2016; Dewey, 1934). I use the term "penetrated" to capture the dynamics of experience that includes being taken in by the experience. That is, how being (a felt experience of experience) and the environment (forces of the experience that include human and non-human, all matter) interact in unanticipated ways to bring forth learning. In this way, learning is not situated only in the mind, as in reflection, to cognize; nor only in the body, as trauma; nor only in the heart, as emotion. The mind-heart-body sensing is compelled to learn by undergoing, having, being taken by an experience. I use the pronoun "we" to signify the mind-heart-body-human-nonhuman-nature-material forces that undergo experience.

Dewey elucidated that ongoing completions of experience (i.e., learning processes) are not final or fixed ends, "for they shed meaning along the way" (Dewey, 1934, p. 26). When we undergo an experience as a relationship that is recurrently savored with special intensity, it points the way to a new knowing of possibilities and potentials. Dewey (d'Agnese, 2016), who was early to the posthuman discourse, described in his pragmatics that when we undergo an experience that makes way for the letting go of anticipation and allows the multiplicity of possible potentials to emerge, paradoxically, then we learn through the unknown (Nicolaides, 2015; Yorks & Nicolaides, 2013) that gives shape to a hope-full future. Dewey, praised as the father of adult learning in the American Pragmatist milieu, introduced this liminal potential of undergoing experience as the ground from which adult learning emerges. The concept of undergoing learning receded into the background after Follett's mention in 1924, until it was regenerated by poststructuralist philosophers in the late 1990s and early 21st century (Barad, 2007; d'Agnese, 2016; Semetsky, 2003). Situating adult learning as part of the process of undergoing experience allows encounters with the unknown to be penetrated.

Dewey (1916) elaborates:

[M]ere activity does not constitute experience.... Experience as trying involves change, but change is meaningless transition unless it is consciously connected with the return wave of consequences which flow from it. When an activity is continued into the undergoing of consequences, when the change made by action is reflected back into a change made in us, the flux is loaded with significance. We learn something. (p. 146)

Dewey (1934) describes the circulation of dynamic forces in undergoing experience as a requirement for critical reflection and new learning to take shape. In *Art as Experience* (1934), Dewey suggests releasing one's energy as a way of reflection. Without removing what has been deeply placed in our souls, there can be no freedom for us to perceive, act, and "summon our energy to be responsive" (p. 55). Notably, the precondition of freeing energy is possible when we reach a state of reverie. If our imagination is constrained, "the subconscious fund of meanings stored in our attitudes have no chance of release" (p. 287). Thus, undergoing is only possible through surrendering oneself, allowing new meaning and learning to emerge. In *Democracy and Education*, Dewey describes the nature of experience:

The nature of experience can be understood only by noting that it includes an active and a passive element peculiarly combined. On the active hand, experience is trying a meaning which is made explicit in the connected term experience. On the passive, it is *undergoing* [emphasis added]. When we experience something, we act upon it, we do something with it; then we suffer or undergo the consequences. We do something to the thing and then it does something to us in return: such is the ironic combination. The connection of these two phases of experience measures the fruitfulness of value of the experience. (1916, p. 63)

Mary Parker Follett, Carl Rogers, Lev Vygotsky, and Paulo Freire gave a central place in their theories to the relationship between experience and the experiencer. All these theories imply that adult learning is a process of experiencing experience that shapes multiple responses. My research into adult learning reveals a way of knowing that exists in the territory where the ironic combination of experience and response is latent—that of generativity. In this territory of the experience of experience, gifts are given as patterns of meaning emerge to create understanding that becomes a "tuft of grass" (Nicolaides, 2008) long enough to steady insight as it becomes a guide for response. I use the metaphor *tuft of grass* to connote the latent, already-thereness of insight that becomes real as it emerges to greet one "like a miracle becoming manifest." It is like walking a marsh, not able to see beneath the muck, and yet there is sure footing that rises to greet you so that you do not sink into the murkiness (Daloz, 2012).

Generative knowing is ways of being and becoming that creatively liberate potential that is always unfolding in the intra-active combination of experience. Generative knowing is dynamically intra-active, an inter-penetrative sensing of multiple possibilities becoming, that do not have to originate in a human self. Bateson (1991) described epistemology as follows: "the stuff of knowledge is always made of the news of difference . . . the next step from news of single differences is to the building of patterns or configurations" (p. 233). The logic of generative knowing is becoming through unfolding metaphors, the evolutionary stuff of adult learning (Nicolaides, 2015) that allows different possibilities to be revealed, critiqued, and nourishes guidance for meaningful response-able action.

Adult Learning Concepts in Dialogue

Putting theory in dialogue is a way to listen differently to what learning can become. In the following section I am in dialogue with generative learning from the cognitive science point of view, primarily the work of Wittrock

(1992). I then listen into the conceptualization of triple-loop learning to better understand the dynamics of learning in action primarily through the works of Torbert (2004); Tosey et al. (2012); and Bateson, (1972). I am the lineage holder of these concepts that help me to theorize a different path for adult learning to take flight.

Wittrock (1992) introduced generative learning theory in the field of educational psychology. In a departure from learning as behavioral conditioning or simple recall of facts previously encoded, he proposed that learners actively generate or construct meaning of ideas and concepts by relating them back to prior knowledge and experiences (Mayer, 2010; Wittrock, 1992). Generative learning theory is rooted in a constructivist epistemology (Tobias, 2010). Wittrock's work is concerned with how individuals learn, but it mostly ignores context and ontology. Wittrock (1992) identifies four processes for generative learning: attention, motivation, knowledge or perception, and generation. The learner actively selects what information or knowledge will receive attention (Mayer, 2010; Wittrock, 1992). The learner then generates meaningful relationships among concepts, and between new concepts and prior experience and knowledge (Wittrock, 1992). The emphasis is on reorganizing and reconceptualizing as learners generate new meaning, rather than passively recording knowledge for later recall (Wittrock, 1992). The implication for training and instruction is the creation of containers for learners to engage in active meaning-making, rather than emphasizing lecture and memorization of facts and knowledge (Yorks & Nicolaides, 2013). Generative learning theory suggests that such generative learning strategies allow for the transfer of learning to new learning tasks and new situations (Mayer, 2010; Tobias, 2010). From an epistemological perspective, Wittrock's (1992) generative learning theory is rooted in constructivism. Constructivism involves reflection on distinct experiences by individuals with an aim toward producing or constructing new knowledge and meaning (Fenwick, 2000; Merriam & Baumgartner, 2020). This approach to experiential learning informs Wittrock's approach to learning and instruction in generative learning theory.

Early in my research (Nicolaides, 2015; Nicolaides & Lim, 2020), I (re)defined generative learning as "a 21st-century learning capacity, concerned with actualizing personal and societal potential through adults learning interdependently (connected with all things that matter, alone and together), consciously connected to head, heart, and body, for mutual and transforming benefit" (p. 3). It is worth noting a few facets of this definition. One aspect is the identification of the current timeframe in human history as relevant. The 21st century is placing demands on learners due to increased volatility, uncertainty, complexity, and ambiguity (VUCA). I have argued (Melacarne & Nicolaides, 2019) that the traditional instrumental learning approach, where knowledge acquisition for problem-solving is privileged, will no longer suffice. As I have been thinking about generative learning, I contrast a knowledge society (where individual knowledge and skills are key to change), with a learning society (where the degree of complexity presents challenges that cannot be resolved by individuals in isolation). Thus, generative learning acknowledges this context of complexity and the need for a different theory of adult learning to meet a 21st-century world replete with thorny, interrelated challenges.

As I have continued to think about generative learning, my focus is not simply on learning new knowledge or skills, but also on building or expanding the learner's capacity. *Capacity* refers to the complexity of meaning-making (Nicolaides, 2015; Nicolaides & McCallum, 2013; Yorks & Nicolaides, 2013). Another useful distinction found in this definition is the linking of the individual and the broader context. This seems to indicate a more enactivist epistemology, where individuals and the environment are co-emerging (Fenwick, 2000). In fact, out of my dissertation research (Nicolaides, 2008, 2015), generative learning is described as "learning that interacts creatively 'in-the-person' and 'within-reality' to generate a changed world" (Nicolaides, 2015, p. 180). Similar to John Heron's notion of ontology as subjective-objective, the interpenetration of the person with the cosmos (Heron, 1992; Heron & Reason, 1997), such a stance is necessary, given complexity that cannot be resolved individually, alone. I speak to this interdependence and connectedness as being requisite for adult learning as a process of transformation. That is, learning is not an activity in isolation of one's social, historical, and cultural context. Speaking to head, heart, body, matter, nature, provides a more holistic approach to learning that is just as concerned with our way of being as it is with our way of knowing and doing. In fact, it is the aspect of being that might prove critical in connecting triple-loop learning (Torbert et al., 1972) to generative learning. The word "potential" is also worth emphasizing in this definition of generative learning, as potential is hidden within complexity (Nicolaides, 2015; Pendleton-Jullian & Brown, 2018). By creating conditions for potential to emerge, there is an opportunity for mutual learning and transformation for both individuals and systems. I have further elaborated on this thinking to fold in the idea of transformation in mind as "catalyzing new perspectives that engage and lead to radical innovation and rapid transformation in the face of continuous disruption" (Melacarne & Nicolaides, 2019, p. 40). It is worth highlighting that generative learning also appears in organizational learning literature. Chiva and Habib (2015) distinguish among zero, adaptive, and generative learning. They view zero learning as simply internalizing, or as Scharmer (2018) might say, downloading existing processes, norms, and knowledge. They argue that adaptive learning is an improvement to the existing order of norms, knowledge, and objectives. They refer to this existing order as the explicate order building from Bohm's work (1980; cited in Chiva & Habib, 2015). The explicate order is the manifested order that we see in the world. Chiva and Habib (2015) contrast this with the implicate order where "everything is connected and enfolded into everything else" (p. 3).

Generative learning involves seeking the implicate order so that new explicate orders can unfold. Chiva and Habib (2015) link their analysis to Bateson's (1972) work on levels of learning. Specifically, they identify generative learning as having to do with Learning Levels II and III. As I have muddled through the epistemological threads of adult learning theories and stumbled into my own notion of generativity, I have found that generative learning is yet another way to reproduce systems of power that become habits for action. Adult learning theories reflect the paradox of liberatory education and reproduction of structures of power (Habermas, 1985). The desire for liberation is coupled with the voluntary endurance of oppression as a habit of action. Deleuze and Guattari understand the mutating forms of desire as per the changes in the means of production through their new ideas—*deterritorialization* and *reterritorialization*. Desire means valorization of objects; however, if desire is a movement and a force, it should be free from a fixed position. In this sense, deterritorialization refers to the process of freeing desire from the fixed point (Holland, 1999). Somehow this process aligns with decoding, as it involves the erasure of meaning that was once attached to the object. Reterritorialization, in contrast, refers to stabilizing the movement into other fixed points. In other words, it means linking desire to different objects, or designating meaning to the new objects. The process of reterritorializing adult learning in its liberatory ontology through my research revealed multiple possibilities as a dynamic more akin to generative knowing than generative learning. Thinking with the concept of generative learning allowed me to find this new understanding of earlier research following the phenomenon (Freeman, 2019) of ambiguity and its learning potentials (Nicolaides, 2008).

Triple-loop Learning as a Form of Generativity

Triple-loop learning is a concept that is mentioned in the literature but seems shrouded in mystery. Even discussions by leading thinkers leave the reader simultaneously intrigued and confused. In many ways, triple-loop learning appears magical or spiritual in nature (Peschl, 2007; Torbert, 2004). In fact, Torbert's (2004) action logic, which engages regularly in triple-loop awareness, is referred to as the Alchemist or Magician. Even the origins of triple-loop learning in the literature are disputed (Kwon & Nicolaides, 2017; Tosey et al., 2012). Examples of triple-loop learning in the literature are scarce and are often quite vague in terms of linking examples to tangible theory (Starr & Torbert, 2005). Lastly, while triple-loop learning is conceptually powerful and robust, it is not strongly empirically validated (Kwon & Nicolaides, 2017; Tosey et al., 2012). Still, triple-loop learning has been one way to think about generative knowing.

In their writing, Argyris and Schon (1974) highlight single- and double-loop learning. Argyris (1991) utilized the analogy of a thermostat to differentiate between single- and double-loop learning. As a thermostat reacts to changes in the ambient temperature based on the temperature to which it is set, it engages in single-loop learning. Speaking anthropomorphically, the thermostat is adjusting its behavior based on observation of the outcomes. If the thermostat were able to question why it is set at a particular temperature, it would be engaging in double-loop learning. Double-loop learning thus involves questioning the underlying strategy, values, or logic of the system (Torbert, 2004; Tosey et al., 2012). While it might seem sensible to assume that triple-loop learning originated with Argyris and Schon, a review by Tosey et al. (2012) of the origin and possible conceptualizations of triple-loop learning points out that the phrase itself is a relatively recent addition to the literature, with Hawkins (1991) seeming to pioneer it. Tosey et al. (2012) go on to identify three distinct conceptualizations of triple-loop learning:

a) a type of learning that goes beyond single- and double-loop learning and is superior in that it aims to change the underlying principles or paradigms that undergird the system
b) a type of learning equivalent to deutero-learning. Deutero-learning is defined as being able to carry out or reflect upon single- and double-loop learning
c) a type of learning springing forth from Bateson's Learning Level III

Viewing triple-loop learning as inspired by Bateson's work is most compelling, the rationale being that the first conceptualization seems to equate loops or levels as something to be ascended, with higher being better. Such a broad statement seems to be insensitive to context and learner needs. It also seems to indicate that once graduating from a lower level or loop, one can jettison that learning. Such a claim fails to consider the recursive nature of learning and the adult developmental theory idea of transcend and include (Kegan, 2000). On more critical inspection, the second conceptualization appears simply to equate triple-loop learning with the ability to critically reflect and enact single- and double-loop learning. Argyris (2003; cited in Tosey et al., 2012) defines deutero-learning as meta-learning on first- and second-order learning. Bateson's (1972) articulation offers something different than reflecting on prior loops of learning, while not claiming superiority of that learning.

Bateson's work spanned several fields, including communications, anthropology, and epistemology (Tosey & Mathison, 2008). It is his work on the latter, and specifically around categorizing learning, that is most applicable to exploring triple-loop learning. Bateson (1972) outlines five levels of learning ranging from Zero Learning to Learning Level IV. Bateson identifies Zero Learning as instances where there is little to no change from a stimulus. Instead, the learning here is marked by reception of external information and habituation in response—that is, there is no correction of errors (Bateson, 1972). This fits well with Chiva and Habib's (2015) notion of Bateson's Zero Learning and with Scharmer's (2018) idea of downloading.

Learning Level I assumes that there is a different response provided to the same contexts in different time periods (Bateson, 1972). For Bateson, context, and markers of context, play a significant role in learning. He describes Learning Level I as a change within a set of available alternatives. That is, there exists an opportunity to correct errors within a given context, without ever transforming the context. This level of learning seems much more in line with the concept of single-loop learning. The thermostat adjusts but does not question its underlying beliefs or assumptions. If Learning Level I is predicated on choosing from within a set of alternatives in similar contexts, then Learning Level II is about change in the set of alternatives considered and the recognition of the context within which one is operating. This idea fits well with double-loop learning, where the thermostat considers altering the set temperature rather than simply kicking on once the room temperature is in error. Continuing with the example, the thermostat might adjust throughout the day, to conserve energy, or to the patterns of occupancy. Bateson (1972) described Learning Level II as a change in Learning Level I, and likened Learning Level II to the concepts of learning to learn or transference of learning. Here, meaning-making within context becomes central. Tosey et al. (2012) highlight that by distinguishing the role of context in giving meaning to behaviors, learning must be viewed as recursive and relational. Bateson (1972) highlights this punctuation of human interaction as necessarily involving the individual transacting with his environment. Tosey and Mathison (2008) sum this up by pointing out that Learning Level II occurs when "a new meaning evolves and is enacted in such a way that the person differentiates between past and present contexts" (p. 20).

Bateson (1972) opens his section on Learning Level III with a caution that this level of learning "is likely difficult and rare even in human beings" (p. 20). Further, he notes that such learning may be beyond language itself. There is a noted difference in Level III, as something more than another epistemology, but rather as also involving ontology, the learner's way of being. Bateson (1972) speaks to this as a "profound reorganization of character" (p. 20) and a "profound redefinition of the self" (p. 22). Triple-loop learning "is a total re-creation of oneself as entangled with all matterings" (Kwon & Nicolaides, 2017, p. 91). I have described triple-loop learning as a dynamic figure-ground shift of being (Nicolaides & McCallum, 2013). The selfhood, therefore, that is made through engaging in Learning Level II may no longer serve as the central point of focus (Bateson, 1972). Such description is in line with Cook-Greuter's (2014) language of ego awareness that is exhibited at the Magician or Alchemist stage of adult development. Returning to the idea of context, Bateson (1972) views Learning Level III as learning to perceive and act in contexts of contexts. Put another way, the corrective change is made from a system of sets of alternatives. Keeping with the view that these levels of learning are recursive and interdependent rather than the view that higher is better, Bateson (1972) cautions that such learning may prove dangerous, even psychotic. Tosey and Mathison (2008) point out that Learning Level III presents organizations with the potential for either transformation or revolution. The latter might serve up a set of alternatives that "are likely to abandon, transcend, or overthrow the acceptance of contexts" (p. 23). On a personal level, Bateson (1972) cautions that engaging in Learning Level III learning may lead to a collapse of one's selfhood or identity. In the context of today's crises—a global pandemic and new variants of COVID-19 unfolding; economic disparity in the United States becoming more prevalent; disorder around the world, including recent news that the Taliban have taken over Kabul, Afghanistan, after 20 years of the U.S. military buffer to construct a more democratic functioning government; the United States' preparations to send forces to join NATO in the Ukraine, whose nationhood is under threat from neighboring Russia; and the Omicron COVID-19 variant, which rages on throughout the world)—I cannot help but think that Bateson's caution, though meritorious, is also an invitation to challenge the very notion of selfhood and the (de)centering of identities that are no longer complex enough to hold multiple potentials of becoming.

Triple-loop learning is more than just learning about single- and double-loop learning. By bringing these aspects of learning to life in a powerful and simple way, while also building from Torbert's (2004) work on collaborative developmental action inquiry (CDAI), I describe triple-loop learning as being rooted in ontology (Nicolaides & McCallum, 2013). Here we highlight single-loop learning or inquiry as being mostly focused on our doing as we examine or correct our behaviors considering outcomes. Double-loop learning or inquiry is focused on our knowing as we examine our strategies, underlying beliefs, and driving assumptions, while of course also encompassing our doing at the single-loop level. That being so, triple-loop learning is concerned with our being and our willingness or openness to reconfigure our intentions and purposes (Nicolaides & McCallum, 2013) to deterritorialize our meaning schemes and reterritorialize our ontology as always in a state of becoming with all matterings. Such a view fits well with Peschl's (2007) articulation of triple-loop learning having to do with our existential self. Similarly, Scharmer's (2018) Theory U brings attention to the core self, our being. Of course, this view also fits well with Bateson's (1972) description of a pronounced reorganization of the self at Learning Level III.

Torbert (2004) articulates the impact of triple-loop feedback as "increasing our awareness of the still vaster volume of inchoate, implicit possibilities and incongruities in each moment" (p. 10). Relatedly, Scharmer (2018) highlights the power of redirecting our attention toward the interior, the source. Peschl (2007), too, makes much of the quality of "one's attention and receptiveness" involved with accessing one's existential domain. After reviewing triple-loop learning, one might be willing to give more grace to the scant examples of triple-loop learning in the literature, which almost always seem mystical, fuzzy, or enigmatic. This level of learning is not something with which many appear to engage individually or collectively (Torbert, 2004). Peschl (2007) makes compelling arguments for triple-loop learning as essential to profound change. What if profound change were already here and what was required was a new attunement to the sensation of an ever-unfolding possibility? Thinking with triple-loop learning gives me more confidence to claim generative knowing as a nomadic theory of adult learning— that is, learning that comes from beneath our perceptions and in the space between the intra-actions of ever-unfolding potentialities.

Evolving Adult Learning

By weaving connections across adult learning theory, I reveal that facets of adult learning theory result in some productive and much reproductive action. Adult learning is the driver for adult education, the method for the aspiration to a more just, inclusive society. As a theory, adult learning is a force to galvanize in service of a goal, a wish, an aspiration. Generative knowing is less of a force and more potential, freed. Paraphrasing Andrew Barry's quotation from Deleuze and Guattari (1987), the intent was and remains to recognize and release a multitude of "whole other stories vibrating within" the claims and arguments of a theory.

In dialogue, generative learning, triple-loop learning, and incidental learning reveal that learning is dynamic, ever-changing, a power to wield. What new inquiry arises from the desire for adult learning to make things different (affirmative ethics) for self, systems of organization, society, nature, when this aspiration is paradoxically liberating and confining? Adult learning has voluntarily been appropriated as a mechanism for reproduction when its ethics are to critique and disrupt in order to keep the habit from forming, to remain true to multiple possibilities and their consequences. Generative knowing comes from troubling the paradox of the desire for more justice for selves and society (human and more-than-human), and that learning also does not change things it desires.

Uncovering a Nomadic Theory of Adult Learning: Generative Knowing

Generative knowing: ways of being and becoming, liberating potential creatively has a triple aliveness: embedded and embodied in mind, heart, body, and matter; entangled with the unknown in all present moments; a gift given and received. This nomadic theory of learning inquires beneath experience, where the sensations of experience are vital in the dark luminous territory of the unknown. Generative knowing emerges from a kind of inquiry that frees potential, becoming actualized in complex responses that create new realities (Deleuze & Guattari, 1987). Generative knowing posits an ongoing inquiry of what might become from an experience with the unknown. What might we co-create with the unknown? What ethical response-able action is galvanized through the complexity beneath the already intra-active intertwining of self and society?

Generative Knowing: Ways of Being and Becoming that Activate Potential Creatively

To be a nomadic theory is to make conscious use of displacement (of not being at home or of being between homes) so that new subjectivities, spatialities, and temporalities might be marked and produced in spaces of betweenness that reveal the limits of their productions of knowledge inseparable from—if not completely absorbed in—the mess of everyday life. Nomadic theory is not a distinct body of theory, but rather a way of doing theory differently, of working inside out, of fugitive moves and emergent practices interstitial with productions of knowledge. Working in this nomadic way allows different questions to emerge that make a theory celebrating distinctions, while also moving in ways that may alter the constitution and constructions of theory

(Katz, 2017). This book is a making of a theory from the subject of lived experiences that are living in me.

My approach to theorizing has been to cut, weave, thread, entangle, and submerge multiple ontologies that allow generative knowing: ways of being and becoming activating potential creatively. The main method for doing this is to follow the ontology of experience, a methodology I will discuss further in Chapter 3. Embodying a stance of receiving, being, and becoming with multiple subjectivities that I have encountered and lived through—as a daughter, as an accompanist, as a researcher, as a scholar, as an activist, as an educator, as a friend, as a deep inquirer—I reveal generative knowing that activates potential in me, primarily. The chapters of this book unfold as stories revealing colorful cartographies, connecting and crisscrossing lines of life that uncover the territories of generative knowing: ways of being and becoming activating potential creatively. Generative knowing is potential given; receiving potential is the subject of the chapters that follow.

References

Argyris, C. (1991). Teaching smart people how to learn. *Harvard Business Review, 69*(3), 99–109.

Argyris, C., & Schon, D. A. (1974). *Theory in practice: Increasing professional effectiveness.* Jossey-Bass.

Barad, K. (2003). Posthumanist performativity: Toward an understanding of how matter comes to matter. *Signs: Journal of Women in Culture and Society, 28*(3), 801–831. https://doi.org/10.1086/345321

Barad, K. (2007). *Meeting the universe halfway: Quantum physics and the entanglement of matter and meaning.* Duke University Press.

Bateson, G. (1972). The logical categories of learning and communication. *Steps to an Ecology of Mind*, 279–308.

Bateson, G. (1991). *A sacred unity: Further steps to an ecology of mind.* Harper San Francisco.

Braidotti, R. (2019). *Posthuman knowledge.* Polity Press.

Chiva, R., & Habib, J. (2015). A framework for organizational learning: Zero, adaptive and generative learning. *Journal of Management & Organization, 21*(3), 350–368. https://doi.org/10.1017/jmo.2014.88

Cook-Greuter, S.R. (2014). *Nine levels of increasing embrace in ego development: A full-spectrum theory of vertical growth and meaning making.* Researchgate. https://www.researchgate.net/publication/356357233

d'Agnese, V. (2016). Undergoing, mystery, and half-knowledge: John Dewey's disquieting side. *Studies in Philosophy and Education, 35*(2), 195–214. https://doi.org/10.1007/s11217-015-9483-2

Daloz, L. A. (2012). *Mentor: Guiding the journey of adult learners (with new foreword, introduction, and afterword)*. John Wiley & Sons.

Deleuze, G., & Guattari, F. (1987). *A thousand plateaus: Capitalism and schizophrenia* (B. Massumi, Trans.). University of Minnesota Press. (Original work published 1980)

Dewey, J. (1916). Democracy and education. In J. A. Boydston (Ed.), *The middle works of John Dewey, 9*, 1899–1924.

Dewey, J. (1934). *Art as experience*. Penguin.

Fenwick, T. J. (2000). Expanding conceptions of experiential learning: A review of the five contemporary perspectives on cognition. *Adult Education Quarterly, 50*(4), 243–272. https://doi.org/10.1177/07417130022087035

Follett, M. P. (1924). *Creative experience*. Longmans, Green and Company.

Freeman, M. (2019). The analytic rewards of materializing the effects of actor-networks. *Qualitative Research, 19*(4), 455–470. https://doi.org/10.1177/1468794118778977

Habermas, J. (1985). *The theory of communicative action, Volume 2: Lifeword and system: A critique of functionalist reason*. Beacon Press.

Hawkins, P. (1991). The spiritual dimension of the learning organisation. *Management Education and Development, 22*(3), 172–187. https://doi.org/10.1177/135050769102200304

Heron, J. (1992). *Feeling and personhood: Psychology in another key*. Sage.

Heron, J., & Reason, P. (1997). A participatory inquiry paradigm. *Qualitative Inquiry, 3*(3), 274–294. https://doi.org/10.1177/107780049700300302

Holland, E. W. (1999). *Deleuze and Guattari's Anti-Oedipus: Introduction to Schizoanalysis*. Routledge.

Katz, C. (2017). Revisiting minor theory. *Environment and Planning D: Society and Space, 35*(4), 596–599. https://doi.org/10.1177/0263775817718012

Kegan, R. (2000). What form transform? Learning as transformation: Critical perspectives on a theory in progress. In J. Mezirow (Ed.), *Learning as transformation* (pp. 35–69). Jossey-Bass.

Kwon, C., & Nicolaides, A. (2017). Managing diversity through triple-loop learning: A call for paradigm shift. *Human Resource Development Review, 16*(1), 85–99.

Maturana, H. R., & Varela, F. J. (1987). *The tree of knowledge: The biological roots of human understanding*. New Science Library/Shambhala Publications.

Mayer, R. E. (2010). Merlin C. Wittrock's enduring contributions to the science of learning. *Educational Psychologist, 45*(1), 46–50. https://doi.org/10.1080/00461520903433547

Melacarne, C., & Nicolaides, A. (2019). Developing professional capability: Capacity and competencies to meet complex workplace demands. Fostering employability in adult and higher education: An international perspective. *New Directions for Adult and Continuing Education, 163*, 37–51. Jossey-Bass.

Merriam, S. B., & Baumgartner, L. M. (2020). *Learning in adulthood: A comprehensive guide*. John Wiley & Sons.

Nicolaides, A. I. (2008). *Learning their way through ambiguity: Explorations of how nine developmentally mature adults make sense of ambiguity*. EdD dissertation, Teachers College, Columbia University.

Nicolaides, A. (2015). Generative learning: Adults learning within ambiguity. *Adult Education Quarterly, 65*(3), 179–195. https://doi.org/0741713614568887

Nicolaides, A., & Lim, A. (2020). Undergoing the experiences of the COVID-19 pandemic as ruptures in American civil society create conditions for right action. *Reflective Practice, 21*(6), 844–860.

Nicolaides, A., & McCallum, D. (2013). Inquiry in action for leadership in turbulent times: Exploring the connections between transformative learning and adaptive leadership. *Journal of Transformative Education, 11*(4), 246–260. https://doi.org/10.1177/1541344614540333

Pendleton-Jullian, A., & Brown, J. S. (2018). *Design unbound: Designing for emergence in a white water world, Volume 2: Ecologies of change.* MIT Press.

Peschl, M. F. (2007). Triple-loop learning as foundation for profound change, individual cultivation, and radical innovation. construction processes beyond scientific and rational knowledge. *Constructivist Foundations, 2*(2–3), 136–145. http://constructivist.info/2/2-3/136

Scharmer, C. O. (2018). *The essentials of Theory U: Core principles and applications.* Berrett-Koehler Publishers.

Semetsky, I. (2003). Deleuze's new image of thought, or Dewey revisited. *Educational Philosophy and Theory, 35*(1), 17–29. https://doi.org/10.1111/1469-5812.00003

Starr, A., & Torbert, B. (2005). Timely and transforming leadership inquiry and action: Toward triple-loop awareness. *Integral Review, 1*(1), 85–97. http://hdl.handle.net/2345/4245

Tobias, S. (2010). Generative learning theory, paradigm shifts, and constructivism in educational psychology: A tribute to Merl Wittrock. *Educational Psychologist, 45*(1), 51–54. https://doi.org/10.1080/00461520903433612

Torbert, W. R. (2004). *Action inquiry: The secret of timely and transforming leadership.* Berrett-Koehler Publishers.

Torbert, W. R., Glueck, E., & Elmering, H. (1972). *Learning from experience: Toward consciousness.* Columbia University Press.

Tosey, P., & Mathison, J. (2008). Do organizations learn? Some implications for HRD of Bateson's levels of learning. *Human Resource Development Review, 7*(1), 13–31. https://doi.org/10.1177/1534484307312524

Tosey, P., Visser, M., & Saunders, M. N. K. (2012). The origins and conceptualizations of 'triple-loop' learning: A critical review. *Management Learning, 43*(3), 291–307. https://doi.org/10.1177/1350507611426239

Wittrock, M. C. (1992). Generative learning processes of the brain. *Educational Psychologist, 27*(4), 531–541. https://doi.org/10.1207/s15326985ep2704_8

Yorks, L., & Nicolaides, A. (2013). Toward an integral approach for evolving mindsets for generative learning and timely action in the midst of ambiguity. *Teachers College Record, 115*(8), 1–26. https://doi.org/10.1177/016146811311500808

THREE

 Following the Phenomenon in Phenomenological Research

WHEN YOU ENCOUNTER WHAT YOU have not yet come to know, how do you respond? I begin feeling like I am treading deep water in the ocean from where no shore is visible, and then, like I am returning home, I continue farther out to sea. As a phenomenologist, I have encountered many awkward situations like the one above when exploring the essential features of the phenomenon of ambiguity. The word has its origins in the Latin *ambi* (both ways) and *agere* (to drive), which led to the word *ambigere* (to waver, to go around) that then grew into *ambiguus* (doubtful), and, in the early 16th century, became the English *ambiguous*. In current vernacular, *ambiguous* means open to more than one interpretation, or having a double meaning, in the sense of obscure, indistinct encounters with language and/or experience. In 2008, I conducted a phenomenological study that began the arc of my inquiry into the ontology of the not-foreknown. I began that study with ambiguity, the ambiguous, as a way to initiate an inquiry into the not-foreknown. I defined *ambiguous* as a mystery hidden in potential. I crafted this definition based on my own experience of the ambiguous territory of my own identities, lived history, and way-making through life that would force me to go around, be doubtful of, and be open to more than one interpretation when encountering the ambiguous. The irony that is captured in the short vignette at the start of this chapter reflects the world of patterns and ideas that seem partly upside-down when one comes face-to-face with the ambiguous. In this chapter I describe situations of crafting a multitude of spaces for exploring the phenomenon of ambiguous that was, in itself, ambiguous. What follows is an exploration of the phenomenological variations that emerged in order to follow and learn from the phenomenon of the ambiguous. These variations led to the uncovering of generative knowing, the subject of this book.

How do you encounter the ambiguous? As a phenomenologist, I asked myself that question to prepare to explore the phenomenon with the nine participants who were inspired to join me in this inquiry for my dissertation study (Nicolaides, 2008). I set out to conduct a phenomenological study, with an approach that Merleau-Ponty (1945/2005) describes thusly: "... in order to see the world and grasp it as paradoxical, we must break with our familiar acceptance of it and, also, from the fact that from this break we can learn nothing but the unmotivated upsurge of the world" (2005, p. xv). He continues: "Phenomenology is an ever-renewed experiment in making its own beginning; that it consists wholly in the description of this beginning, and finally, that radical reflection amounts to a consciousness of its own dependence on an unreflective life which is its initial situation, unchanging, given once and for all" (2005, p. xvi). I found that it was in the awkward silence that ran so deep between the participants in the study and myself that "primary consciousness can be seen appearing not only in what words mean but also what things mean: the core primary meaning round which the acts of naming and expression take shape" (Merleau-Ponty, 2005, p. xviii). In the spaces with participants, we generated and encountered several ambiguous experiences that led us to rediscover our own presence to ourselves. In essence, we did not reduce experience to present the dimensions of the phenomenon, as is customary in phenomenological research; we become known to ourselves through each other from within the ambiguous space between us.

The power of phenomenological texts lies precisely in this resonance that the word can effect in our understanding, including those reaches of understanding that are somehow pre-discursive and pre-cognitive (not foreknown) and thus less accessible to conceptual and intellectual thought (Van Manen, 1990). The creative contingent positioning of words may give rise to evoked images that can move us: inform us by forming us and thus leave an effect on us. When this happens, says Gadamer (1996), then language touches us in the soul. Or, as Bachelard puts it, the reverberations bring about a change of being, of our personhood (1964, p. xviii). He says that the image has touched the depths before it stirs the surface (of our being or self). It becomes a new being in our language, expressing us by making us what it expresses; in other words, it is at once a becoming of expression and a becoming of our being. Here expression creates being (Bachelard, 1964, p. xix). Phenomenology formatively informs, reforms, transforms, and performs the relation between being and practice (Van Manen, 1990). It was from within a space between the co-inquirers and me that a performance emerged as a way to create ambiguous being, so that we could encounter ambiguity in action.

This study was shaped by the phenomenon's unfolding to "have its say" (Freeman, 2011). The space in which it appeared was through deep and vulnerable conversations. Such an approach implies and accepts the constraints of an inter-subjective dialogue as methodological boundaries to explore and make sense of the ambiguous. Gadamer (1989) described a *conversation* as an evocative space in which the essential features of a phenomenon can emerge:

> A genuine conversation is never the one that we wanted to conduct ... it is more correct to say that we fall into conversation, or even that we become involved in it ... a conversation has a spirit of its own ... the language in which it is conducted bears its own truth within it—it allows something to "emerge" which henceforth exists. (p. 383)

Gadamer (1989) emphasized the value of meaning-making conversations involving both researcher and participant engaged in a shared encounter with ambiguity. Responding to the study's research questions required conducting a probing, detailed investigation into the nature of our encounters within ambiguity. In this research, the participants and I shared lived encounters with ambiguity and co-constructed the meaning of our experience. In order to follow the phenomenon, the participants and I had to surrender to the ambiguous unfolding itself in the space between us.

As a way to initiate the ambiguous, I performed a three-act play that made visible my encounters with the ambiguous dimensions of my own life as a woman with multiple identities. The performance became a space for conversation, which helped the participants and me to surrender to the ambiguous and "let it have its say." Here I present the three-act play that I wrote and performed with each participant, followed by a discussion of the phenomenological variations that emerged with each participant.

Ambiguous three acts:

One woman, myself, plays all the characters representing the lived ambiguous throughout her up-till-now life span. I employed dramatization of voice and body language to convey the different characters enacting the ambiguous identities held within me.

There is a stool in an empty space in the middle of a room, and light that shines on the stool. The play unfolds around the stool.

I-in-beginning
(My own voice)

Raised on two islands; one in the Mediterranean sea and the other in the straits of Malacca, born in a hospital in an American Midwestern city. The smell of lemons, the taste of rose water, the impossible azure sky above and sapphire sea below . . . a living history unforgiving, unforgettable; a living reality forming, re-forming . . . becoming

ACT I
The Kitchen
Agios O Theos . . . (*Holy God* speaks Tenor father)
Kalimera . . . (*Good morning* speaks Soprano aunt)
'Siopi . . . oooft pia' . . . (with bitterness in her voice, *Silence!* speaks Yiayia)

Yiayia (grandmother)
Soldiers came knocking at our door . . . it was siesta time, sacred and not to be interrupted, quiet time the whole city experienced . . . too early for coffee, the shared nap-waking ritual of the nation . . . . The gun was pointed at my heart . . . this was the last time I saw my home.

Aunt
Living in the old city felt crowded and exhilarating at the same time. Everyone was moving along the thousand-year worn cobblestones that led to so many hidden seen places . . . most importantly places for me to be seen . . . . I was after all the Queen of the old city . . . ask anyone . . . they will tell you . . . "Sophia! Oh yes I remember her . . . first woman to own a car, her own business at 18 teaching piano and ballet and married into a good family . . . . I detest bombs . . . they create so much dust . . . . I do not know what the fuss is about anyway . . . . I am not of the dust, I am of royalty, must be protected . . . .

Father
Without warning the big sounds of bombs falling and striking. The sound burned my ears as the bombs opened in our shared courtyards; the church walls and the thousand-year cobblestones . . . . I was scared . . . .

I remember the sight of one part of our home destroyed under the rubble and across the courtyard my brother and I huddled under a mattress . . . to protect us.

ACT II
The Veranda

All politicians are blind . . . they cannot see farther than their desire for power . . . you think they care about us . . . they do not even know where our homes are on a map . . . accept it . . . the world is ruled by the privileged and they are the all-powerful . . . stupid fools, you are wasting your time Ahx . . . . Let's talk about the soccer match, that should cheer us up . . . is there more coffee? pass me the nuts . . . .

We are to blame . . . we gave them our lands, our homes, our loyalty like fools . . . we are idiots...we deserve this . . . My God! Why can't you stop talking about the past. Enough! Forget about home, it does not exist but in your imagination . . . wake up!

So there was a man and a woman . . . recently married . . . arranged that is . . . and their families were curious to know about their sex life . . . so one evening they sent one of their sons to listen at the door . . . this is what he reports he heard:

Allah! Ou Akbar (*God is great*)
Allah! Ou Akbar (*God is great*)
Yaret! Ou Akbar (*if only you were bigger*)

Maria . . . you know how to tell a joke even under the worst circumstance . . . did you hear about the rubber bullets flying across the sky . . . they killed the woman who used to sew for us . . . they said she posed a threat to security . . . My God! This watermelon is so sweet . . . where did you get it . . . from the gypsies?

ACT III
The Rubber Trees

Sticky . . . that's how it felt leaving the plane, meeting the humidity wall that assaulted me coming down those steel steps—the Goddess Guardian days of my playground tribe, now dust behind me while this tropical island grabbed the inside of curls once long and luscious turned to a tangled gnarl.

Everyday there was a new curve to learn on the always growing changing streets of this tropical island state. So many threads, so many stories on top of one another . . . a nation was being built and I was watching . . . while my own nationality was dissolving . . . I was becoming a body departing from the cozy ground of somebody.

Cultural genetic interweaving . . . marriage . . . threading desperate abandoned swaths of fabric become a wedding dress. On the rose mountain, I get a ring on my finger. Followed by tropical island baby-making. Then, divorce. A public state, affairs, eyes wide open. Riding rollercoaster tracks of my brittle life.

The hardened rubber sap gracefully pours on, live.

The play catalyzed the conversations that ensued over a year of encounters with the participants in this study to make visible, felt, heard, sensed, the ambiguous. In the following discussion, I present the methodological variations that began with the framing of the study followed by what emerged as methods of reflection *within-the-ambiguous*, free from theoretical, prejudicial, and suppositional intoxications. Phenomenology is also a project that is driven by fascination: being swept up in a spell of wonder, a fascination with meaning. That intoxication led to freedom to let the ambiguous "have its say."

Phenomenon: The Ambiguous

Complexity denotes the interconnectedness, interdependency, and unprecedented rate of change occurring in the social field (Boulton & Allen, 2007; Cilliers, 1998; Shaw, 2006; Stacey & Griffin, 2005). *Complex ways of knowing, doing, and being* refers to an individual's developmental (cognitive, affective, and interpersonal) capacity to make meaning, adopt various perspectives, and engage in intelligent action (Cook-Greuter, 2004; Kegan, 1994; Nicolaides, 2015; Nicolaides & McCallum, 2014; Torbert, 2004). The absence of predictability and order characterizes the complex liquidity of this period of early 21st-century life that leads the ambiguous encounters of life (Bauman, 2007; Snowden & Boone, 2007). Complexity science has demonstrated that complex adaptive systems generate the seeds of their own transformation, in which learning represents "the continuous improvisations of alternate actions and responses to new possibilities and changing circumstances that emerge" (Fenwick, 2003, p. 8). To explore the ways and the extent to which individuals encounter the ambiguous generated by liquid modernity, I sought individuals who possessed complex ways of knowing, doing, and being (Kegan, 1994; Torbert, 2004). Complexity gives rise to the ambiguous when traditional, predominantly rational responses to learning are inadequate and challenged. Seeking to understand the lived experience and felt-sense of the ambiguous, I inquired: How do you encounter the ambiguous?

A few words about more complex ways of knowing, being, and doing as the selection criteria for my participants: My rationale for selecting participants with more complex ways of knowing was twofold. First, I assumed that adults with more conventional and less complex ways of perceiving abstract experiences would describe encounters with the ambiguous as events to be avoided, or that they might even be unable to identify such encounters. Second, I assumed that adults with more complex ways of knowing, doing, and being would have the cognitive, affective, and interpersonal capacity required to engage and describe complex and abstract phenomena that are ambiguous. Since my dissertation study, I have changed my mind about the need for complex ways of knowing, being, and doing as a way to activate the potential that the ambiguous holds. In the chapters that follow, I will work with the richness of life told in stories that activated generative knowing in my being and becoming. However, it is useful to explore how this methodology, of listening to stories, is a portal to moving beneath lived and living experience.

As Mikecz (2012) notes, access to participants can be a challenge. As a novice researcher, while conducting my dissertation study, I set out to recruit participants in a conventional way, by developing a clear research summary and inviting participation from a group of adults with more complex ways of knowing. That strategy was deadening to my study; no one took up the invitation. I realized that if I sought to inspire adults to join in my research, I had to demonstrate what I knew of the phenomenon and its impact on me. Aesthetics, I find, encourages me to encounter dimensions of myself I am unaware of or have forgotten. This inspired me to write a three-act play, which I shared above. By writing the play I made public my own encounters with the ambiguous (Benz & Shapiro, 1998; Harvey, 2011; Van Manen, 1990). Since a phenomenological approach allows the researcher to explore with respondents the meaning of significant dilemmas in their lives, this play enacted my lived encounters with the ambiguous dimensions of my life, exposing my own vulnerability and doubtfulness. I displayed my vulnerability in my willingness to go first, so to speak, in exploring my own way of encountering the ambiguous, remaining open to the unknown potential that this exposed vulnerability would stimulate in the audience.

A mutually intuitive selection and developmental invitation in the form of a play were used to attract the nine people who joined me in my inquiry. These nine adults who became curious about exploring the ambiguous with me gifted me with the beginning awareness of what I now describe as generative knowing: ways of being and becoming. I performed my play as a way to be seen in my own raw exposure of living the ambiguous. The vulnerability on display became the base from which we began to have conversations about the ambiguous in our lives.

Given the demands of the inter-subjective meaning-making endemic of a phenomenological study (Dahlberg & Dahlberg, 2020; Maxwell, 2005; Madison, 1981), it is evident that the relationship between the participant and the researcher is part of what becomes explicit in the research (Mikecz, 2012). This relationship requires attending to the care of participants who hold the living meaning of experiences and who are not to be treated as a "tool to extract data" (Maxwell, 2005, p. 84). Lawrence-Lightfoot and Davis (1997, p. 137) argue that "relationships that are complex, fluid, symmetric, and reciprocal—that are shaped by both researchers and actors—reflect a more responsible ethical stance and are likely to yield deeper data and better social science." I highlight these distinctions in order to emphasize the rationale for the selection process, particularly because I actively involved myself in the meaning making process with participants.

Eliciting the Phenomenon in the Moment

In the conversation with participants, the initial semi-structured set of probing questions—which were designed to prompt reflection, description, and conversation *about* ambiguity—elicited thin responses. It became apparent that asking participants to recall past experiences of ambiguity was not yielding interesting descriptions. When our attention shifted from attempting to describe past experiences of ambiguity to meeting the ambiguous in our conversations, this led to the encounter with the ambiguous within our exchange. A little taste of this encounter follows below:

Participant: Did we exhaust ambiguity in my answering of your question? Seems too soon to me.

Researcher: *Remains silent*

Participant: Let's be silent together.

Researcher: *Beginning to get choked up; feeling fear of failure, then disappointment, then inner quiet.* I am feeling very quiet inside, afraid that there is nothing of interest when exploring the ambiguous, and I do not know what comes next . . . .

Participant: (interrupting) There, here it is, now here an ambiguous moment we share.

This exchange illustrates the unique quality of the conversations. Our conversations began with a performance of my three-act play, moved into a discussion about the play's impact on the participants, then on to reflection-on-past-lived-experience that was ambiguous, which then ended abruptly as each participant began to question the point of exploring the ambiguous. It was in those moments of confrontation—in a space occupied by my own uncertainty about how to proceed and the participant's intuition—that what emerged from the horizon of our encounter was at first ambiguous. From within that moment of recognition, that we were ambiguous, the opening invited us to deeper inquiry and mutual discovery. Our intuitive and developmental steadfastness through these ambiguous conversations let the phenomenon have its say. Phenomenology accepts that reality is my experience of reality, and that it is valid. Merleau-Ponty (Madison, 1981) describes this as a philosophical method of perception:

> The phenomenological world is not the bringing to explicit expression of a pre-existing being, but the laying down of being. Philosophy is not the reflection of a pre-existing truth, but, like art, the act of bringing truth into being. (pp. xxii–xxiii)

The illustration above shows the making of meaning within ambiguity that emerged within the conversations.

In Pursuit of the Ambiguous

Each conversation space created with the participants was unique. No single approach was replicable across each conversation. The performance of my play generated a relational space by making public my own vulnerability with the ambiguous aspect of my identities. An emic code emerged through the data which described this conversation as "mutuality may be the highest mystery." This quality of phenomenological conversation gave way to mutuality that lends shape to the ambiguous, as illustrated and discussed through our experiences in the vignettes I share below.

In this research, an emphasis on the mutual construction of meaning arose (Bourdieu, 1977; Giddens, 1986). At many junctures of our conversations, participants solicited my own lived experiences to help make sense of their own, in effect using one another to shape meaning of the ambiguous that was arising between us. The ambiguous had a voice because of the unique relationships formed between the participants and me. These intimate relationships developed because I willingly exposed my vulnerability and the rawness of encountering the ambiguous dimensions of my living identities. I share vignettes of the unique ways this phenomenological conversation became the source of rich data for this research.

Ambiguous Integrity

As a novice researcher at the time of this study, I was overwhelmed by the demands placed on me in the space of intimate relationships with the participants that ensued as the very method of making space for the ambiguous. Paradoxically, the more willing I was to be seen and to be emotionally intimate with these individuals, the more they were willing to surrender their ability to protect themselves from intrusion (Hunter, 1995), as will be illustrated in the descriptions below. As you read the vignettes, notice the complexity of our relatedness where vulnerability and intimacy activate the ambiguous (Mikecz, 2012).

Jane came to discover after her wedding night that her then-husband was transgender, eager to try on Jane's lingerie and desperate to be a woman. Jane jumps into the conversation with her hands making a kind of fist and says it was like "getting knocked down, and the getting back up was big for me" was Jane's way into the ambiguous in her life. She was young when she married her best friend, sure that this was her soul mate and true love. Discovering his secret was shocking and made her desperate for escape. Yet she endured this ambiguous time in order to remain true to herself. She made visible her integrity by standing within the ambiguous choices her then-husband was struggling with, to be a man, to be a woman, to be married to his best friend. Here is how the ambiguous gave her voice:

Jane: The point is that working out what is the correct action, or however you want to put that, or the right path. That's essential for human beings to do, and that sometimes you choose that path even though you're not going to like it. Lots of things you won't like, and at the same time you may be wrong. Of course, that's an ideal that's hard to live up to. I'm not denying that, and I miss it [the path] all the time. I'm sure we [she and her husband John] would both have said that, but we both shared a deep discomfort with certainty—philosophical, particularly, and religious, and political with certainty.

Jane asked me what held me steady when I encountered ambiguity. I shared:

Researcher: One of the things that's striking me is that I both invite and rescind ambiguity. It challenges my integrity . . . like you say it's hard to live on the path without becoming ideological . . . having firm knowing . . . What I feel is a different kind of presence, that when I am true within ambiguity I am more honest and willing for the path to find me when I miss it . . . ambiguity shows up and messes the path up while also putting me back on it....

Our co-inquiry led Jane to communicate that when she encounters ambiguity "the point is not working out what is the correct action . . . but rather taking myself seriously in a moment when the color of life leaves me." In the above exchange, as Jane and I leaned into making meaning together, we shared the realization that our sense of integrity was the steadiest structure to rely on in the discomfort of our encounters with ambiguity. Ambiguity catalyzes an encounter with ourselves as we are, which is uncomfortable, especially when what is revealed challenges our self-concept. A reframing spirit arises within ambiguity inviting a humble inquiry into how to act from a sense of personal integrity.

To further illustrate the texture of phenomenological conversation, I offer a segment of conversation between Nigel and me.

Nigel: I guess I'm an arrested two-year-old because I only know things when I put them in my mouth. I take people for walks in the woods and they say, what kind of a tree is this? And I pull it out and chew a little bit and tell them what kind it is.

Researcher: [laughs] Oh, yeah, that's a eucalyptus tree.

Nigel: You can tell that one. [laughs]

Researcher: I've been thinking a lot about the kind of things that emerged in our previous conversation. Here's my observation: that in our conversation, I feel like we are walking through treacherous territory holding hands . . . .

Nigel: Uh-huh.

Researcher: Encountering this piece of something called ambiguity. That we were approaching it from the top and from the bottom and from the side and through our language, trembling on the tips of our toes.

Nigel: Yeah.

Researcher: ... we are tentative in pursuing a little bit deeper to find out more and I thought, wow, isn't that interesting, I feel like we are the ambiguity looking at ambiguity.

Nigel: ... for a lot of folks, there's enormous ambiguity. They're dealing much of the time with ambiguity, and the metaphor of a swamp is very helpful in their understanding, how do you move through a swamp? We look in swamps and we talk about how swamps aren't all water. They usually have some little tufts of grass, or little hummocks that are dry and you can kind of stand on those while you look around and see where you're going to move next. It's important to recognize the role that swamps have, not simply as a negative thing, but, in fact, wetlands are an extremely important part of the large ecology because they purify the water, and they recharge the aquifers and have a number of important roles in the environment that inform how you think about working in the swamp-like conditions that you're in at work and in life. So, I think of how we work with ambiguity to create or come up with metaphors to help us understand ambiguous circumstances. A good, rich metaphor can provide a map through an ambiguous situation. It's a metaphor that helps us negotiate the ambiguity of our inner life. A good metaphor is tentative and robust ... gives you that kind of tentative operating stance.

Researcher: I am resonating with the notions of robust tentativeness and creative imagination. Those are the things that I want to taste more and take in ... there seems to be some truth about the need for a new way to be or live in the movements of ambiguity that demands we pay attention differently, language differently.

Nigel: Beautiful. It's really, that's nice, beautifully spoken...where the movement that takes place, because beneath language certainly isn't lack of movement. There's movement beneath language, maybe that's where most of the movement is. In fact, I think probably language and thought stabilize movement and channel it in ways that allow us to feel as though we have some control over our lives. So, the paradox is that where the real deep movement is, there is a new language.

As the inquiry unravels in the conversational exchange between a participant and myself, you can listen to the murky use of language giving shape to ambiguity, leading us to recognize the movements beneath language as we peek at the mystery within ambiguity.

Without the authentic quality of mutual inquiry, the seemingly unknowable mystery of ambiguity cannot be known; only when the participants and I look together does the richness of the inquiry become revealed.

Ambiguous Mutuality

One of the conundrums of engaging in inquiry with participants is negotiating the power dynamics between researcher and participant (Mikecz, 2012; Plesner, 2011). I had inoculated a more conventional sense of power—I, the lowly researcher gaining access to these nine extraordinary adults, and they offering me enormous amounts of time to inquire with me—by performing the play I wrote. The space that opened up between those unique adults and me was filled with another type of power that I was challenged by: mutuality. Mutuality emerges as a genuine partner in a relationship where both parties know nothing and have nothing in advance that the other wants. Mutuality invites a raw form of inquiry demanding from the inquirers discernment moment by moment of their willingness to remain faithful to the mystery without being too quick to claim its gifts or run away.

In the conversations with Alex, the challenge of mutuality was felt and explored. Alex, a powerful white man, interrupts our conversation:

Alex: I am bored with our conversation at this moment. You must have more ways to engage me, what is the next act?

Researcher: I am not sure what you mean? What act?

Alex: Your performance intrigued and attracted me. This conversation does not. Forced ambiguity is a killer.

Researcher: My next act is to let you know that I am now afraid of you and intimidated by you. I feel shut down and simultaneously angry at your arrogance and voyeurism. I am not here to perform for you. WE are here in your home, amongst your things, in a place where you are in control, seeking the ambiguity that may arise in the space between us. At this moment I feel powerless and my shields are up!

Alex: Ah ha! Power . . . I was wondering when that was going to come up. You took up your power so fully in your performance and yet here I experience you as awkward and want to assert my power. How might we restore a power between us?

Researcher: *Breathing deep a few times . . .* feeling a little wobbly . . . I need courage in this moment and I ask that you see how your power moves in the moments before were just that: power moves that come with privilege.

Alex: Well said and named. I accept my bad behavior and regret my initial stance. I see now that we need to drop into some mutual space. How?

Researcher: Can we sing a song together? How about row, row, row your boat?

We sing together and begin to laugh.

Alex: start here. Mutuality may be the highest mystery. Mutuality wouldn't be a problem if we were completely specified and equal, because, if we were already specified and equal, there'd be an equation of some sort for mutuality, whatever it was. It's precisely because we're different and not equal that mutuality is a constant mystery. In other words, what it means to be mutual . . . listening inside and outside to find out what is truly mutual is ongoing and is mysterious, and as soon as you think you know it, then you stop listening, and then you become unjust.

In the above exchange, you can catch a glimpse of the danger and mystery of ambiguity. The strange dance of forms of power eventually led to a kind of mutual inquiry. In the space of our power-full inquiry, Alex described ambiguity as holding the keys to mutuality when he said "mutuality may be the highest mystery." The time I spent with Alex was most uncomfortable, and upon reflection, I was grateful for what emerged with some difficulty and imbalance (Plesner, 2011). This encounter captures well why working with elite participants is so difficult and so rewarding. The demands placed on a researcher in such a moment are a test to the strong container that a researcher must generate for deep inquiry to take shape. In my case, my long preparation and research design involved a great amount of intra-subjective exploration in order to find the courage to be vulnerable with both the participants and the phenomenon (Mikecz, 2012).

Learning Within Ambiguity

Of great interest to me was the question of why mutuality played such a significant role in the process of learning about ambiguity. Alex elaborated further on the concept of mutuality in the experience of our interviews as he read the transcripts of the first conversation. He remarked on how our conversation seemed to demand a confrontation of ambiguity from both of us. The discussion below illustrates how we had to quickly learn about a mutuality that could hold us long enough to inquire together into the mystery of ambiguity.

Alex: What came to my mind [reading the transcript of our first interview conversation] was a kind of exercise of power. If you divide consciousness between dependent and independent and my new favorite term, inter-independent, and say that power, as we traditionally know it, is almost entirely associated with the dependent orientation, then I want to link those three orientations to past, present, and future, where the dependent orientation is oriented toward the past. So, unilateral power is power that has an immediate visible effect. You can tell it just happened because, you know—I asserted my privilege unilaterally in our first conversation and you felt it and named it. So, unilateral power is the most visible power and, for people whose knowledge is oriented to the past, it's the only kind of power they can see or appreciate, really, and since the world that we see created in front of us is a world that was created in the past, all of its symbols, or most of them, point toward forms of accumulated power in the unilateral sense.

Researcher: Seems to me that mutuality is a demanding power that at first is a power struggle . . . before there is an acceptance of our mutuality, it opens us to willingly begin a process of constructing some new shape of power we determine in the moment . . . as we did after we sang together . . . .

Alex: [continues] . . . the inter-independent orientation is, first of all, more present-oriented, and then instead of having sort of fixed images of the future, it sort of feels the potential of the future. It, in a sense, cascades many potential meanings for the future, but rooted in the present and that's the least visible form of power because it's creating new imagination of what power can be, or what anything can be, what people can be, what states can be when people are mutual . . . giving their unilateral power away and accepting the possibility of a mutual sense of power.

Researcher: . . . a mutual sense of power seems to be a rare form of being together.

Alex: True mutuality is both co-created and co-generated. It is the ultimate of possibility . . . uncommitted potentiality for change. Eventually, mutuality took shape after a kind of struggle for power and forced ambiguity . . . when we began again an inquiry within a mutual resonant and co-generated ambiguity.

From my encounters with Alex, I learned the demands that ambiguity places on me before the mystery is revealed through a cascade of meanings. As a qualitative researcher, the relationship between participant and researcher is delicate. The willingness to engage the tensions that ensue when there is inevitable unevenness in such a relationship influences the quality of data. I learned in my encounters with Alex that I, too, had unilateral power that I exercised in the moment of confrontation before I could surrender to a greater ambiguity within mutuality. The enormous amount of data I collected through hours of conversation and interactions was daunting. I struggled to find ways to organize and make sense. Once again I had to surrender to the path of ambiguity and accept what it revealed as a path to sense-making.

Making Sense of No-Sense

In organizing the data I struggled to find suitable phenomenological data reduction methods. I settled on developing narrative inquiry profiles and rigorous coding that led to thematizing thick descriptions of novel features of ambiguity (Charmaz, 2014; deMarrais, 2004). As Atkinson (2005, p. 10) points out, "narrative is not a unique mode of organizing or reporting experience, although it is one pervasive and important way of doing. Narrative is an important genre for spoken action and representation in everyday life, and in many specialized contexts." Narrative inquiry profiles featured each participant's unique encounters with ambiguity based on their lived experience. In essence, each profile became a way to present one-person plays of the participant's encounter with ambiguity. Upon completion of these profiles, I shared them individually with each participant to produce further thematic analysis. With permission, I then invited participants to read and reflect on each other's profiles, generating further data analysis that led to the identification of novel descriptions of encountering the mystery within ambiguity (Grbich, 2013).

Bringing the narrative profiles, the rich thematic descriptions of novel features of ambiguity, and engaging in shared analysis generated a collage-like effect, unifying seemingly disparate fragments of meaning. Within this collage, thick descriptions capturing unique features of encounters with ambiguity served as the primary analytic units. A synthesis of descriptions resulted in another level of collaborative analysis that crystalized novel features of the phenomenon of ambiguity and encounters with the mystery that lies within. This collaborative analysis and continued meaning-making process with elite participants prompted additional insights:

Veronica: Oh! And let me not forget the whole entire conversation being a play of "I know, you know, I know . . . ." Unveiling the "you know"—the wizard is exposed behind the curtain by the playful absentmindedness of Toto in

Oz. That this entire interview reveals my own "you know." The "you know" of inquiring vulnerability and of making sense from moment to moment that is leaving behind the knowing instrument of the intellect and evoking the knowing of being—intuitive, present, and in a state of alert relaxation. It occurs to me that in the space of our conversation what is revealed is us sitting behind the curtain speaking into the mechanism that exaggerates our being rather than be our being. I feel the humility and the revelation of my own exaggerations.

Researcher: Is it possible to be intimate with the unknown?

Veronica: That is the nature of our particular encounter—intimate being with each other in our unknowing and within ambiguity.

The process of engaging with the participants in thematic identification and discussing their meanings with play-like narrative displays was part of the unfolding subjective stance of this research. These approaches with these elite participants enhanced the quality of analysis eliciting deep understanding of these data.

Conclusion and Discussion

By grounding my inquiry in an approach that is epistemologically philosophical, I created the conditions for a form of deeply subjective and inter-subjective research to take shape as a direct way of understanding and describing ambiguity. This research yielded the richest descriptions, not in the reported statements of one person, but in what emerged in the mutual understanding that two or more persons reached through following the phenomenon wherever it took us to have its say. This novel approach accepted the complexity of reflexive conversation and mutual meaning-making (Alverson & Skoildberg, 2004), making space for ambiguity to take shape. A first-person approach would dictate that the subjectivity of second-person research would be removed and reported as third-person objectivity without the complex dimensions of an inter-subjective interaction where the phenomenon was actually experienced. Wanting to preserve the subjective, because that is where ambiguity appeared, I found myself engaged in an approach different than what conventional qualitative research demands. The participants and I fell into a mutually vulnerable conversation that made space for ambiguity to take shape and shape its meaning and us.

In the context of my study, and in this book, I use intuition and essence as interchangeable features of descriptive language identifying the features of ambiguity and the forms of encounter that generated learning. This methodology facilitates a description of "knowledge as it appears to consciousness, the science of describing what one perceives, senses, and knows in one's immediate awareness and experience" (Hegel; cited in Moustakas, 1994, p. 26). When I began this study from a distance, I was afraid of my own encounter with ambiguity and what it would reveal that I did not want to see or know. The phenomenon pulled me into the vulnerable inner space of meaning and experience with my participants that was unplanned and unpredictable by my performing a three-act play of that vulnerability. By allowing this novelty to unfold, trusting that the participants and I would collectively grow new abilities of inquiry while we encountered ambiguity, we allowed for a more "sufficiently complex, accurate, nuanced, and mutually shared understanding" (McGuire et al., 2007, p. 125) of the phenomenon. This chapter depicts the ambiguous pursuit of ambiguity by following the unfolding of the phenomenon itself as a method for uncovering generative knowing. I was fortunate that I found a way to engage with extraordinary people that involved a high level of vulnerability and interactive conversations that moved beyond traditional researcher-participant relationships and, in the process, evolved into a deeper, richer exploration that may only be possible when we meet each other on new ground that is shaped by the unfolding of the phenomenon where our mutual gaze constructs meaning within the ambiguity itself.

In the chapters that follow, I extend this method of inquiry to uncover the potential that generative knowing activates. The stories in each chapter are a relatedness that I explore in the ways that generative knowing is activated in me: through *Ruptures* in knowing, by *In-scending* beneath the story and language of certainty to uncover mystery; and by receiving awareness that is active, what I language as "*Awaring.*" Chapter 3 features generative knowing that arises from my personal lived experience, while Chapters 4 and 5 bring alive generative knowing by inquiring into stories I heard repeatedly throughout my life, uncovering potential that had previously remained hidden. Chapter

6 is the work of one of my graduate students, who has taken up generative knowing in her research and writes about her lived experience through the lens of generative knowing as her way of activating being and becoming. In writing this book I have become aware that I am giving voice to a form of knowing that has been elusive and yet always present when I began to inquire beneath my own experience of experience. The next chapters attempt to give this knowing—which I call generative—shape, form, and power.

References

Alverson, M., & Skioldberg, K. (2004). *Reflexive methodology: New vistas for qualitative research.* Sage.

Atkinson, P. (2005). Qualitative research—Unity and diversity. *Forum Qualitative Sozialforschung / Forum: Qualitative Social Research,* 6(3).

Bachelard, G. (1964). *The poetics of space.* Penguin.

Bauman, Z. (2007). *Liquid times: Living in an age of uncertainty.* Polity Press.

Benz, V. H., & Shapiro, J. J. (1998). *Mindful inquiry in social research.* Sage.

Boulton, J., & Allen, P. (2007). Complexity perspective. In M. Jenkins, V. Ambrosini, & N. Collier (Eds.), *Advanced strategic management: A multi-perspective approach* (2nd ed., pp. 23–47). Palgrave.

Bourdieu, P. (1977). *Outline of a theory of practice.* Cambridge University Press.

Charmaz, K. (2014). *Constructing grounded theory* (2nd ed.). Sage.

Cilliers, P. (1998). *Complexity and postmodernism: Understanding complex systems.* Routledge.

Cook-Greuter, S. (2004). Making the case for a developmental perspective. *Industrial and Commercial Training,* 36(7), 275–281.

Dahlberg, H., & Dahlberg, K. (2020). Phenomenology of science and the art of radical questioning. *Qualitative Inquiry,* 26(7), 889–896. https://doi.org/10.1177/1077800419897702

deMarrais, K. (2004). Elegant communications: Sharing qualitative research with communities, colleagues, and critics. *Qualitative Inquiry,* 10(2), 281–297. https://doi.org/10.1177/1077800 403262359

Fenwick, T. (2003). *Learning through experience: Troubling assumptions and expanding questions.* Krieger.

Freeman, M. (2011). Validity in dialogic encounters with hermeneutic truths. *Qualitative Inquiry,* 17(6), 543–551. https://doi.org/10.1177/1077800411409887

Gadamer, H. (1996). *The enigma of health: The art of healing in a scientific age.* Stanford University Press.

Gadamer, J. (1989). *Truth and method* (J. Weinsheimer & D. G. Marshall, Trans.). (2nd ed.). Crossroad.

Giddens, A. (1986). *The constitution of society: Outline of the theory of structuration.* University of California Press.

Grbich, C. (2013). *Qualitative data analysis: An Introduction*. Sage.
Harvey, S. W. (2011). Strategies for conducting elite interviews. *Qualitative Research, 11*(4), 431–441. https://doi.org/10.1177/1468794111404329
Hunter, A. (1995). Local knowledge and local power: Notes on the ethnography of local community elites. In R. Hertz & J. B. Imber (Eds.), *Studying elites using qualitative methods*. Sage.
Kegan R. (1994). *In over our heads: The mental demands of modern life*. Harvard University Press.
Lawrence-Lightfoot, S., & Davis, J. H. (1997). *The art and science of portraiture*. Jossey-Bass.
Madison, G. B. (1981). *The Phenomenology of Merleau-Ponty: A Search for the Limits of Consciousness*. Ohio University Press.
Maxwell, J. A. (2005). *Qualitative research design: An interactive approach*. Sage.
McGuire, J., Palus, C., & Torbert, W. (2007). Toward interdependent organizing and researching. In A. Shani (Ed.), *Handbook of collaborative management research*. Sage.
Merleau-Ponty, M. (2005). *Phenomenology of perception* (S. Colin, Trans.). (Original work published 1945). Routledge.
Mikecz, R. (2012). Interviewing elites: Addressing methodological issues. *Qualitative Inquiry, 18*(6), 482–493. https://doi.org/10.1177/1077800412442818
Moustakas, C. E. (1994). *Phenomenological research methods*. Sage.
Nicolaides, A. I. (2008). *Learning their way through ambiguity: Explorations of how nine developmentally mature adults make sense of ambiguity*. EdD dissertation, Teachers College, Columbia University.
Nicolaides, A. (2015). Generative learning: Adults learning within ambiguity. *Adult Education Quarterly, 65*(3), 179–195. https://doi.org/0741713614568887
Nicolaides, A., & McCallum, D. (2014). Accessing the blind spot: The U process as seen through the lens of developmental action inquiry. *Perspectives on theory U: Insights from the field* (pp. 48–60). IGI Global.
Plesner, U. (2011). Studying sideways: Displacing the problem of power in research interviews with sociologists and journalists. *Qualitative Inquiry, 17*(6), 471–482. https://doi.org/10.1177/1077800411409871
Shaw, P. (2006). *Changing conversations in organizations: A complexity approach to change*. Routledge.
Snowden, D. J., & Boone, M. E. (2007). A leader's framework for decision making. *Harvard Business Review, 85*(11), 68–76.
Stacey, R., & Griffin, D. (2005). *A complexity perspective on researching organizations*. London: Routledge.
Torbert, W. R. (2004). *Action inquiry: The secret of timely and transforming leadership*. Berrett-Koehler Publishers, Inc.
Van Manen, M. (1990). *Researching lived experience: Human science for an action sensitive pedagogy*. State University of New York Press.

FOUR

Luminous Darkness

IN THIS CHAPTER, I PRESENT the aspects of generative knowing that I described in Chapter 2—*Ruptures, In-scending,*[1] and *Awaring*—through my own personal #MeToo experience. To illuminate these aspects of generative knowing and how they activate learning, I begin by inquiring beneath my own lived experience and deep ontology of a trauma that I became aware of when I turned 19 years old. Since my consciousness of this trauma, I have worked with many different methods of healing and forgiveness to understand and transform the trauma that lives in me. Many aspects of this trauma live quietly in me, feel healed, and the predator is forgiven for his abuse of power. However, as I was approaching my 50th year and entering the mystery of menopause, I began to notice in my meditation practices and quiet prayers that there was a territory in my consciousness I could not access. It felt like I was bumping up against the stone of my existence. I felt that dissolving this stone and finding my way through it was important for how I would enter my crone years. I began a new practice of inquiry, accompanied by a skillful guide who would hold me and my soul energetically as I *In-scended* into the dark territory beneath the experience of my experience of the trauma. It is beneath this lived experience where I discovered how generative knowing would activate a different potential in me by rupturing what I have kept hidden: the sensations I was not ready to receive. When I inquired into my lived experience in this new way, I encountered the *Rupture* of this hidden side in ways that allowed for openings, portals to multiple potentials of my being and becoming. One of these potentials is becoming this book.

Niels Bohr (1963) said that "we are a part of that nature of knowledge that we seek to understand" (p. xii). Attuning to the nature of knowledge(s) that is part of me and yet not fore-knowable is where generative knowing is found. Our ability to know the world hinges on a recognition that we are already part of the knowing that we seek, already entangled with existence. This means that learning and existence are not simply intertwined with one another, as in the joining of separate entities, but rather that each lacks an independent, self-contained existence. Existence is not an individual affair. Individuals do not preexist their interactions; rather, individuals emerge through and as part of their entangled intra-relating across time and space. The experiences that we each have alone and collectively forge meaning. What side of that meaning forging intra-action are we paying attention to? Emergence does not happen once and for all, as an event or as a process that takes place according to some external measure of a particular space and of time. Rather, time and space, like matter and meaning, come into existence, are iteratively reconfigured through each intra-action. This kind of process makes it impossible to differentiate in any absolute sense between creation and renewal, beginning and returning, continuity and discontinuity, here and there, past and future (Dewey, 1934; Barad, 2007). It is a good thing that we have this limitation; it is the ambiguity at the heart of things that saves our weary souls. Without this vitality, learning (formal) is used to discipline, control, and punish. In the end, it is because of our humanity—because of our limitations, because we cannot ever truly know ourselves—that we become.

What if it were possible to rewrite the power of experience so that it creatively liberated potential? What would such a rewriting make in the world? Between the ages of 3 and 12, I was sexually molested by a member of my extended family. I kept it hidden. My own #MeToo. The episodes of molestation happened in a family member's basement, or a dark closet, and sometimes in plain sight. Such is the power of the predator, to seem innocent while he steals innocence. As a phenomenologist, I understand and value the power of intersubjectivity and the authentic entanglement of researcher and subject. My entanglement is with this past experience that I became aware of many years after the lived experience. As I have engaged in an ongoing inquiry about this experience over the course of my lifetime, poking at it from all sides, using all the tools of inquiry and supports available to me, I have felt that there was something that colonized me, and I could not escape that past. As I described above, as I was approaching the age of 50 and entering the mystery of menopause, I began to play with a different inquiry: *Who is the stranger I am becoming?* This inquiry worked me differently in that it led me deeper into the ambiguity of my past experiences that will also be ever-present in me, influencing my future. What follows is the story of generative knowing that uncovered a different truth as I followed the inquiry, *Who is the stranger I am becoming?*

Knowing that I was molested between the ages of 3 and 12 was the first healing. Spending two decades seeking understanding was a second healing, and there was a third healing that I did not seek, but which sought me unexpectedly when I left the seeking behind to experience the sensations of an experience of a sacred ritual of fungi. What found me was a truth that freed me from the tyranny of the trauma, the story of having my innocence stolen.

Since 2006 I have participated in an action inquiry group that practiced attention to first-, second-, and third-person experience as a way to grow and develop the capacity to lead and learn. Members of this fellowship became dear friends over the years. I made plans with some of these dear friends to spend a few days over New Year's (2019) at their home on Whidbey Island (off the coast of Washington State, USA). The third healing that deepened my commitment to write occurred in the liminal space between the end of 2019 and the beginning of 2020, just before the global pandemic took hold of the world. As part of our New Year's inquiry practice, I was invited to participate in the sacred ritual of fungi in the safety of my beloved friends' care and in the beauty of a nearby cemetery nestled in a redwood forest. Reader, you should know that I have been on an intentional path of inquiry about my own trauma (unnatural stillness) since I was 25 years old, practicing many different paths to uncovering and inquiring into the depth of my experience through yoga, exploring different spiritual philosophies, taking refuge as a Tibetan Buddhist, experiencing indigenous therapies for healing trauma through vision quests and psychodrama, talk therapy, bodywork, and homeopathic remedies to heal mind, body, and soul. I want to emphasize that I have been "working on myself" intentionally for many years with committed friends and other friendly accompanists who have supported my desire to encounter the unknown in me. The experience of the sacred ritual of fungi cannot be seen as a one-time, stand-alone, magic experience that broke open a book in me. Sacred rituals of accompaniment in the closeness of knowledgeable friends and a loving friendship brought me deeper and beneath the territory of my trauma in a way different from the ways I was already exploring. The experience of this sacred ritual could not have been fore-known. Also not fore-known was that the journey would take me deeper into the invisible, dark territory of an inquiry I have been becoming friends with over the past 25 years.

I had resisted such invitations before, but now I was surrounded by three trusted friends, including my most beloved life-long friend, in a relaxed natural and social environment. The experience was transformative in ways that continue to unfold in generative ways for me. The effect of the sacred ritual led to a courageous frame-breaking insight: I saw myself keeping one foot in the known and the other in the unknown (locked in-between two worlds). I was bound by a well-worn groove that was no longer so groovy. The insights from the experience of the sacred ritual broke that groove and led me to the invisible world beneath my life experiences in a different way. I moved past what I had been struggling to move through at the bottom of my being where, in my meditation, I would encounter a stone-like cover over my soul that rendered me unnaturally still, unmoving, and somehow not accessing all of myself. That apocalyptic event reconfigured my relationship to this stone cover, melting it and freeing the sensations that were trapped inside. Multiple protective identities were re-ordered. A new landscape from which I could creatively respond emerged from an already there territory that was beyond the unnatural stillness I longed to shake. Until this experience, the sensation of unnatural stillness was one that lived in me, keeping me stuck in the stone of my being and at a distance from fuller potentials of my becoming. This reordering of *what-I-had-come-to-know-in-one-way* life experience gave me tangible, evocative language for what I have been theorizing through my scholarship and research these past 15 years. I recognized that the theory that I had previously expressed as learning through complexity and in my dissertation learning through ambiguity (Nicolaides, 2008, 2015) was a different way of knowing, what I have come to describe as generative knowing. Generative knowing emerged as a "languaging" (Maturana & Varela, 1987) of what I have researched as learning through ambiguity as one of the gifts of the sacred ritual of fungi. The story that I share now is the story of how sensations found me and freed the potential of my being and becoming.

A Rupture Through Terror

Perched on a large rock at the edge of the sea, ready to become the salty sea at any moment, I never knew myself as terrified. "Not afraid of anything" would be an accurate description of me from the outside . . . at any age. I was prone to be on the ready to rescue.

Except that I am acutely aware that I am terrified of cockroaches. In a memory from when I was 8 years old, I recall the terror of the possibility of a sensation of being penetrated from the bottom of my feet regardless of shoes to protect them, or the cozy safety underneath heavy bed covers. There is a waking dream logged in my memory of wanting to get up in the middle of the night to go to the bathroom, but feeling terrified because I can sense that the ground is covered by hundreds of cockroaches. In the dream, I am silently calling out for my sister to come and get me and take me to the bathroom. My sister, two years younger than I, hears me and comes to get me and takes me to the bathroom that is just outside our bedroom door. Her presence makes the cockroaches disappear, and I can go to the bathroom untouched by them, not penetrated.

The dream is also reality; in the morning we recollect the dream-like movements of her hearing my call and us going to the bathroom, her sitting on the edge of the bathtub while I pee, both of us in a dream. This vivid moment in our shared history has become one of the folklore stories of our family and is evoked at times when I like to appear fearless in some encounter within larger family dynamics. That image of me, perched on the rock at the edge of the sea, on the ready to do something very courageous, is *penetrated by an awareness* that I am also terrified. Many of my identities—Warrior, Protector, Over-Responsible, Sui Generis, The General—are counterphobic, meaning I seek out what I fear in the hope of overcoming it. I have become aware of my counterphobic identities as sophisticated constructions by my superego, and I am fond of their amazing capability to keep me secure . . . and surviving an experience that logged terror in me.

What terrified me? To seek an adequate understanding of this part of my experience is to begin beneath the story.

I am always returning to a sensation of penetration. I recoil like a sea anemone at first blush. I feel a dark sensation of being in a state of terror and thrill, each holding me hostage to the other. Terror keeps thrill at bay; thrill keeps terror at bay. A Gordian knot. To tell the story of this knot is to tell the stories of the many tucks and turns that tighten the knot from dream to dream. One stiff turn of the knot came in a waking dream when I was 19 years old. I was contemplating sexual relations with a man who I thought loved me because he followed me everywhere I went and engaged in stimulating intellectual banter with me. The waking dream was about an encounter with terror, this time not about cockroaches, but with the darkness that I was anticipating would be part of such a nocturnal activity with him. I was terrified of the dark. I shared with my soon-to-be lover the waking dream of the terror I felt in my body as I anticipated sex with him in the dark.

In the dream there was darkness, but I was not alone; there was someone else in the dark with me. I had a sensation that though the dark was scary, I was terrified of who was in the dark with me. At age 19 I remembered for the first time that there were dark experiences very early in my life that I was terrified of; I remembered that they had to do with a member of my extended family, and dark spaces in the basement of a family home that my family visited when I was growing up, and the space of a dark closet.

When I recalled out loud the waking dream and the sensation, my soon-to-be lover asked a most peculiar question. *Are you cured of that violence?* Shocked by the question and the thought that somehow this violence penetrated me in such a way that rendered me sick, I put on the fearless identity of Warrior and had sex. To have sex is not to make love. The distinction is important, as the having-sex cut deeper into the terror that lived in my waking dreams. A thawed past seeped into my daily reality and the inquiry *What terrified me?* now had a partial answer: The violence in the dark. An answer that I would silently speak to myself while carrying on.

Carrying on is what I do when I think I am sick, not yet cured of the violence.

Seeking a cure for the violence was, for me, a secret affair, one that demanded multiple identities to enact a life of becoming-Aliki-in-spite-of-terror. The Warrior me, becoming-stuck-in-a-cut, and in service of keeping me safe was, and sometimes still is, the first dominant identity of many first encounters. Were you to have met me at the threshold of Warrior me, the effect was either the thrill of an encounter with something exotic or intimidating repulsion. A clear sign that I was stuck-in-a-cut doing the same (keeping the terror at bay) was my divorce—left by the man who touched the cut in the dark and looked away. That leaving-me made me curious at age 25, motivating a deep intellectual, psychological, embodied, and spiritual inquiry into the terror that ruled me. Identity(ies) has (have) very good curative properties, emitting an invisible and odorless effervescence that, when taken in, will do its (their) job. Keep you safe (but not transformed). As the Warrior, and in many of my forms, I was safe from penetration. Stuck on a plane of imminent vigilance. Always the same and no different. Stuck-in-a-cut, #MeToo.

This is one way to tell the story of molestation. Fluid, agile, temporal across many time-spaces—logged in the cut of my being, a cut that remained, regardless of all the healing, many times. Then, I did something really different.

I am 50 years old. I have 50 involutions into the fractured in-territory, visiting and revisiting the main cut, feeling the cutting off of my becoming, thread and needle in hand. An unexpected surprise during my 50th year was a conscious journey of *In-scending* (intentionally inquiring beneath the cut) accompanied with fungi. I accepted an invitation to receive the sacrament of fungi, with a beloved friend hand in hand. The journey delivered an unanticipated, unexpected, not-possible-to-know-before experience—an experience of undergoing the terror, hand-in-hand with my beloved friend and with all that mattered (past, present, future twisted with life itself). I received the sensation of terror as grace, visited by beauty and aliveness. Suspended in animation, my many identities—the Warrior, Protector, Over Responsible, Sui Generis, and the General—had no choice but to watch a shy Aliki becoming uncoiled from inside the cut. As I became less my identities, and more a vital force, shy and quiet, a vast source of connection, I "foolishly" encountered terror unarmed.

Without any cuts keeping me afraid to touch, I was touched by everything. The kaleidoscopic vibrant color and vivid life of everything that surrounded me reached out to entangle me. I did not recoil. Full anemone, I was in a forest of deep green—touched by ancient trees, and the setting of a beautiful cemetery of an intentional community of care and mutual love. I was drawn in by an especially magnificent tree in the back of the cemetery. Standing back-to-back with my beloved friend, everything in intimate devotion.

The roots in motion stretch out to entwine me, a luminous brilliance of color throbbing through the lifeforce branches, roots with grass and soil, and me at the edge of their reaching. Standing unmoving, in the presence of beauty and aliveness, an assemblage of a fractal sky, breathing earth, luminous tree-roots-soil-branches-leaves, and the sound of aliveness, the stone of my being, penetrated.

At that threshold, terror-of-penetration and being-penetrated, I feel the sensations of terror. I am overcome by the intimate feeling of beauty and aliveness, letting everything feel me. I am ecstatic. Life, real, is me. No cuts or scabs to block life in me, no steel walls or protective identities to keep me safe, no stone covers to block my soul's vitality. Without the armor of 50 years of protective skins, I am in an erotic embrace with life and living—vibrating tree in the gaze before me, living decay barely beneath me, every color and design of living reality in motion, all potential in my fingertips. A virtual place for everything to be actualized. In that slow vast present moment, beauty and aliveness lived me past the terror. The stone at the bottom of the being I knew dissolved, giving rise to a new truth, being and becoming Aliki free from the terror. I felt the terror all the way through, not hesitating at the bathroom's edge, or turning away from the darkness of the night; I broke the seal of terror and let beauty and aliveness in. There I am found by a slow-moving, luminous, silvery vastness where everything is all-ready.

As the effects of the fungi began to wane, laughter rose to my lips, over and over again. Hand-in-hand with my beloved friend, taking in the exquisite unfolding beauty of every living material we encountered. As my feet carried me to my friends' hearth, I felt foolish for the steely judgments I held about the sacrament of fungi, in touch with being afraid to lose control, and grateful that it only took 50 years of life for me to allow for being and becoming to drop out from beneath me. I was gifted with the real sensation of terror. Feeling the feeling of terror, that I could now hold as I was held by the living presence of life itself in everything, I received the truth of my own mystery and liberated a liquid potential: being and becoming Aliki. As the identities came rushing back from their suspended state, on the ready to take on their powers for safety, we encountered a vast luminous territory for being and becoming together. The *Ruptured* opening beneath the terror, *In-scending* allowing the sensation, *Awaring* the cuts to know terror; keep beauty and liveness in me.

The illusion that knowing can be had without the sensations of the present, real, is foolishness I now catch in action. The inquiry *Who is the stranger I am becoming?* is not so strange at all; being and becoming Aliki is 50 years wide, lifetimes deep, and not-yet.

Earlier in the book, I presented the method of following the phenomenon as a process for cutting together the intra-active forces across rhythms of time to map experience in the form of phenomenological cartography. The composition you just read is my own way of presenting a cartography of terror. *Cartography* is a theoretically based and politically informed reading of the present. The reading I offer is of a body that is conscious that it is colonized by terror (what Deleuze and Guattari describe as deterritorialization) in the act of reconstituting terror (what Deleuze and Guattari describe as reterritorialization) as being and becoming Aliki. The language of deterritorialization (Deleuze & Guattari, 1980/1987) is potent as it explicitly denotes the conscious resistance to being made or controlled by a dominant ideology—for example, in my case, that being sexually molested made me bad and that somehow I deserved it because I was a girl, and my punishment was the loss of innocence. A dominant refrain spoken to little girls is that they make men do things to them. Deleuze and Guattari (1994) describe the forces of deterritorialization and reterritorializing as the processes of making something new, such as learning as an act of resistance actualizes potential creatively (Deleuze & Guattari, 1994). Generative knowing is such an act of reterritorialization, a dynamic force that reconstituted my being and becoming Aliki by receiving the sensation of penetration not as terror, but as vital potential.

This is being as it is *lived*, captures the process of vitalizing the real terror that was my experience of sexual molestation between the ages of 3 and 12. Donna Haraway (1988) states that bodies and "objects of knowledge are material-semiotic generative nodes" (p. 595) and that the boundaries of bodies "materialize in social interaction. Boundaries are drawn by mapping practices; 'objects' do not pre-exist as such" (p. 595). Boundaries become closed, fixed, permeable, open, and shift from within; boundaries are very tricky. What Harraway emphasizes is that what boundaries "provisionally contain remains generative, productive of meanings and bodies" (Haraway, 1988, p. 576). In this sense, boundaries, the cut in my story, are also subjects that are intra-active, available to re-making or reterritorializing.

Generative knowing vitalized the terror that lived in me in ways that were keeping the truth of my being and becoming hidden. The truth that innocence was not lost, just hidden in the mystery side (the invisible world) of my experience of trauma. To encounter the hidden mystery that does not seek to be known yet seeks to be sensed becomes generative knowing, a different way for learning to emerge. Learning that is generative does not seek an end; it seeks instead a willing surrender to move beneath the boundaries of experience receiving and activating potential creatively.

At the center of adult learning is the notion of agency (Bandura, 1986). When adults are encouraged to become self-directed, they begin "to see themselves as proactive, initiating individuals engaged in the continuous re-creation of their personal relationships, work worlds, and social circumstances, rather than as reactive individuals, buffeted by uncontrollable forces of circumstance" (Brookfield, 1986). Agency is about response-ability, about the possibilities of mutual response, which is not to deny, but to attend to power imbalances. Agency is about possibilities for worldly re-configurings. Agency is not something possessed by humans (or non-humans, for that matter). It is an enactment. And it enlists, if you will, non-humans as well as humans. In my case, terror also had agency. The agency of *Awaring* the terror—meaning, naming it, not merely becoming aware of it—was a power I did not yet have, a more-than-human intra-action that was intertwined in the luminous darkness of the mystery side of my trauma was waiting for me to have the sensations, not the knowledge, of the trauma. Some people are very nervous about not having agency localized in the human subject, but I think that is the first step: recognizing that there is not this kind of localization or particular characterization of the human subject, and it is the first step toward taking account of power imbalances, not an undoing of it. The principle of justice is one that requires more than human agency. It requires responsibility. In his writing, Derrida (1993) describes justice as a form of responsibility:

> No justice . . . seems possible or thinkable without the principle of some *responsibility*, beyond all living present, within that which disjoins the living present, before the ghosts of those who are not yet born or who are already dead. (Derrida, 1994, p. xviii; emphasis in original)

The concept of responsibility entails being attentive to ways in which we may be re-doing or re-producing injustice, not liberating a response that is just, with each intra-action. Intra-action vitalizes the past and the present and the future; it is always being reworked. The dynamic of being reworked says that the phenomena (in my case the sensation of terror) are diffracted and temporally and spatially distributed across multiple times and spaces, and that our responsibility to questions of social justice has to be thought about in terms of a different kind of causality. Generative knowing in this way troubles conventional habits of learning to question the re-production of structures or de-construction of components that are more complex and mysterious as a shorthand to justice. Generative knowing—that is, ways of being and becoming activating potential creatively—is an approach to learning that brings attention to the complexity of intra-actions that are all-ready in order to vitalize response-able potential for self and society. In this sense, agency of self is becoming more just, mutual, and inclusive; agency of society is to reorder its structures to enact that justice. This is the promise of adult learning: to make justice real through learning. The reality of our 21st-century world wants learning that can actualize this promise, and generative knowing may be one such way of learning.

In the next two chapters, you will read the stories of generative learning that emerge in the experiences of reterritorializing my relationships with my parents, Martha and Ari, by listening to them tell the stories of their traumas in ways that make something different in me— what I discover as the stories work me differently, making something different, a vitality that works across generations. An additional story is one of a graduate student taking up the theory of generative knowing to reterritorialize her relationship to the future of work. Read and listen for stirrings that signal generative knowing in you. That is the sensation of being and becoming.

Note:

1. *In-scending*: a word of my own making, meaning to inquire beneath experience, the territory of the unknown.

References

Bandura, A. (1986). *Social foundations of thought and action: A social cognitive theory.* Prentice-Hall.

Barad, K. (2007). *Meeting the universe halfway: Quantum physics and the entanglement of matter and meaning.* Duke University Press.

Bohr, N. (1963). *Essays, 1958–1962, on atomic physics and human knowledge.* Interscience Publishers.

Brookfield, S. (1986). *Understanding and facilitating adult learning: A comprehensive analysis of principles and effective practices.* Open University Press.

Deleuze, G., & Guattari, F. (1987). *A thousand plateaus: Capitalism and schizophrenia* (B. Massumi, Trans.). University of Minnesota Press. (Original work published 1980)

Deleuze, G., & Guattari, F. (1994). *What is philosophy?* (H. Tomlinson & G. Burchell, Trans.). Columbia University Press. (Original work published 1991)

Derrida, J. (1994). *Specters of Marx: The state of the debt, the work of mourning, and the new international*. Routledge.
Dewey, J. (1934). *Art as experience*. Penguin.
Haraway, D. (1988). Situated knowledges: The science question in feminism and the privilege of partial perspective. *Feminist Studies, 14*(3), 575–599. https://doi.org/10.2307/3178066
Maturana, H. R., & Varela, F. J. (1987). *The tree of knowledge: The biological roots of human understanding*. New Science Library/Shambhala Publications.
Nicolaides, A. I. (2008). *Learning their way through ambiguity: Explorations of how nine developmentally mature adults make sense of ambiguity* (Publication No. 3327082) [Doctoral dissertation, Teachers College, Columbia University]. ProQuest Dissertations Publishing.
Nicolaides, A. (2015). Generative learning: Adults learning within ambiguity. *Adult Education Quarterly, 65*(3), 179–195. https://doi.org/10.1177/0741713614568887

FIVE

 A Single Story is a Dangerous Narrative

A single story is a dangerous narrative.

I am of my mother, but my father is honored by the taking of his name and the putting aside of the mothering lineage that gave seed a place.

To tell another story, to re-order a story, to (un)story a story, for only one narrative is a dangerous thing.

The story of seed takes place in fertile home, becoming what its seeding desires; many potentials. One story is too dangerous when fixed in time and in the words of one storyteller. Breaking the story while telling it may be closer to what the old bards did before the story was put into stone.

The stone becoming narrative is dangerous.

No one stone is the same, no one narrative either. Even when the story is told the same way every time. There are multiplicities locked in stones, remembering differently as stones skip across the molten surface of living.

The *Rupture* is not dangerous. It is how wounds heal, truth flowing before it becomes another stone, for another telling.

—A. Nicolaides, In a flash: Metissage, June 2021[1]

SHE IS THE MOST BEAUTIFUL woman in Jerusalem. That is the first story of Martha. Martha is my mother. A woman born in between worlds and times when some things that were true were kept hidden. A woman born in between nation-states and geopolitical redrawing of boundaries. Born in 1946 in Jaffa during a brief time when Jordan was the protectorate of Palestine[2] after the departure of the British, under whose mandate Palestine was protected after the fall of the Ottoman Empire's 400-year rule. Martha, raised in Nablus and schooled in Jerusalem, was a boarder from age 6 to 18 at the Pensionnat de Notre Dame de Sion School and Orphanage for Girls in the Old City of Jerusalem. The school was one of the oldest and most respected educational institutions for girls in a land where education was a prized opportunity

Figure 5.1. The Most Beautiful Woman in Jerusalem

and respected for all, regardless of religious or class affiliation. Muslim and Christian girls were taught by the sisters of Sion.[3] Martha thrived on and excelled in learning, graduating at the top of her class in 1965. She told of the pranks she played on the nuns, along with the other two musketeers, her best friends, Odile and Nora. Their favorite prank was to make the nuns terrified of the cranky old elevator, now a permanent feature of Pontius Pilate's Palace—a place of biblical judgment. As the nuns would walk into the elevator, draw the iron filigree door closed and press the button for up, the three musketeers would rush to turn off the power to the elevator, then so easily done with a flick of a switch, rendering the elevator motionless in mid-space and the nun passengers in furious terror. It was 1965 when Martha graduated from high school, a moment in the history of Palestine that was brewing with foment beneath the routine of school, family, and play that was then still possible on the streets of Jerusalem. Dame de Sion was home during the week, and over the weekend the girls would go back to their homes in Ramallah, Nablus, Bethlehem, Jaffa, Jericho, and in between villages and nearby countries. If the cobbled streets of Jerusalem could tell their story, one would be the well-worn path that Martha walked from the Ecce Homo on Via Dolorosa to her father's pharmacy at Jaffa Gate, or her great grandmother's apartment near the Church of the Holy Sepulcher in the Christian Quarter. The school closed in 1967 at

A Single Story is a Dangerous Narrative

Figure 5.2. Three Musketeers

the onset of the Arab-Israeli Six-Day War. The history of her time at school has been erased. The stones tell stories; stories not to be erased.

A feminist does not at first identify as a feminist out of the traditional ground of her ancestry. By feminist, I mean different (Gay, 2014; Lorde, 2020), on the margins of what is recognizable. A feminist becomes a feminist because she knows that she holds difference and is different. Martha found herself on an unknowable grand life adventure and accidentally became and then raised inconvenient feminists to meet a volatile world. As an Asia-Minor-Greek woman born briefly under the protectorate of Jordan after the British Mandate had abandoned Palestine, Martha becomes a displaced woman, never to return home. Her difference as a displaced Greek-Middle-Eastern woman makes her, and by extension her daughters, feminists. Her living story is the stuff of experience that I explore to create spaces of possibility where new potentials are actualized. I practice aspects of generative knowing to *Rupture* the frames I held in place that knew my mother in one way, *In-scending* to inquiry into the invisible side of her life experience in the stories she tells so that I may make a new story, not to be erased.

Generative knowing is what I describe as a form of adult learning that activates potential through ways of being and becoming. Generative knowing is a way to animate the vital energies that are all-ready in the intra-active space of self and society. The stuff that makes new reality from the potential that is all-ready, invisible, and not-yet in the vitality of being and becoming. What makes new realities? This inquiry is familiar and echoes loudly in the epistemologies that galvanize different ways of seeking answers through philosophy, ecology, quantum physics, spirituality, pragmatism, behaviorism, humanism, constructivism, and all the sciences that forge the knowledge we seek to know. Adult learning is framed as a force of change in the context of adult education and change sciences, a promise to evolve and enact the democratic values and beliefs meant to catalyze a shared global commons where mutual flourishing is liberated (Daloz, 1991; Jarvis, 2011). After years of inquiry into the way ambiguity, an aspect of complexity, might serve as a portal to potential, I have settled on a truth that is wrapped in a more nomadic adult learning theory: generative knowing. Generative knowing offers a way to enter spaces of possibility beneath the stuff of experience, across time and space, at a rhythm that is timeless, to make something new with the stuff that is all-ready and not-yet. Stuff is the language of the invisible world, the material that is in the experience of experience, beneath the known territory of learning or knowledge acquisition. In this chapter I practice aspects of generative knowing, *In-scend* (inquiry beneath the experience of experience into spaces of possibility) by working with the stuff of my mother's stories that I have known in one way, opening to *Awaring* (making something new) potential that was shrouded due to my own well-grooved frames of reference that would not budge until they would. Frame breaking paradoxically demands both volition and relatedness. The intra-active entanglements of timelessness, narratives held like stones, frame braking inquiry, and new meaning-making that names only after sensations of truth emerge. In this chapter, I trace these moves as I hear a story my mother tells in pieces over the course of her lifetime, before, during, and after the Six-Day War, heard all at once in a new way, makes something different. A story not erased.

Narratives Held in Stone

I remember the period of our family's life in Singapore (1979–2001), when my mother had a very active life in Singapore's then-nascent charity-building community. She was involved with multiple community-building projects that she initiated or was invited to collaborate on because of her enduring involvement with the local community. As a long-standing resident of Singapore, and especially during the period between 1987 and 2000, she was involved in multiple community-building activities reported by local magazines and newspapers. A story my mother told many times was her unique experience of living through the Six-Day War while growing up in Palestine. I thought it strange that this story would frame her identity as a community-builder in a country far from her own. She was devoted to Singapore's becoming. We moved to Singapore from Greece in 1979 at the beginning of Lee Kuan Yew's[4] vision of Singapore becoming a center of commerce, where flourishing intersections of global identities were being woven into the construction of a city-state that would become a global economic center. We watched this new becoming of a city-state take shape from the balcony of our apartment.

As I was preparing to write this book, I wanted to return to the stories that framed my mother's life, and especially the story that I had heard or read in some form or another in the many articles that were published about Martha's acts of charity. As I read the articles that my mother collected over the years and kept in a box, I noticed that the story served as a kind of anchor from erasure. I was curious about this and interviewed my mother in January 2020, just before the pandemic came roaring into our lives, curious to hear her tell the story again.

Generative knowing is a process of fluid allowing; to come into contact with the unknown, to allow the possibility of an exchange that occurs beneath the experience of experience that becomes a knowing at a rhythm of its own. In the case of Martha, her experience of living through the Six-Day War is storied many times, each time to liberate a different sensation of knowing that I have come to understand in the writing of this chapter. My mother comes from a line of strong women going all the way back to the Byzantine Empire, when fire and war(s) brought my great-great-grandmothers to their feet—feet that took them from stone to stone, from Constantinople to Damascus to Jerusalem, keeping the family safe with the only currency that was movable

Figure 5.3. Martha Committed to Singapore's Becoming

in those days—family walking hand in hand, and the few gold bangles (if they were lucky to have a few) in their brassieres, as a guarantee.

What Is Experience?

Dewey's theory of knowing influences my understanding and thinking about the experience of experience. *The Quest for Certainty, a Study of the Relation of Knowledge and Action* (1929), as well as *Logic: The Theory of Inquiry* (1938) and *Art as Experience* (1934), are especially good companions as I quest into the concept of the experience of experience. For Dewey, meaning refers to the relationship between things. Understanding the meaning of something is to grasp its position and relationship in the experience, being able to perceive the modification or consequences involved that yields knowing that cannot be fore-known. Things gain meaning when they are used as a means to bring about consequences, or as a means to prevent the occurrence of undesired consequences, or as standing for consequences for which we have to discover meaning. The relation of meaning-consequence is at the center of all understanding (Dewey, 1938).

Understanding, or grasping meaning (of a thing, an event, or a situation), is explicitly defined by Dewey as "to see it in its relations to other things: to note how it operates or functions, what consequences follow from it, what causes it, what uses it can be put to" (Dewey, 1938, p. 137). The acquisition of meaning—i.e., learning—is that of forming "habits" of direct understanding, of apprehension. Meaning comes from all directions. The thing, the event, the situation, the unfolding insight as the experience of experience invites you in.

Accepting the invitation from the experience of experience, to have an experience, is a practice not well described in the world of adult learning, yet it was labeled by Dewey early on as *undergoing experience, to have it* (Dewey, 1934). The assumption is that the experience itself is not enough to bring about learning; to be educative, as Dewey describes it (1938), demands that you undergo it. To learn from experience from a distance rarely becomes transformation (Mezirow, 2000; Hoggan, 2016). To experience the experience of experience takes practice, a willing encounter with *Ruptures* in meaning-making. By *Rupture* I mean the cascade effect of a frame-breaking, like small death of truth held fiercely. The raw recognition that the frame is wrong is difficult. Freeing meaning from the desire of fore-knowing demands radical vulnerability, the willingness to discover something new that may illuminate a different truth. *In-scending* is an aspect of generative knowing involving the practice of leaning into the *Rupture*, moving beneath the experience of experience, to have it, to undergo it.

In listening to Martha's telling of her experience of the Six-Day War— conversations I overheard or articles I read, once they were published, about her charity activities—a little new detail was revealed each time. The different tone or emphasis that came with each re-telling is the stuff that has *Ruptured* my firm knowing and that I am willing to *In-scend* through the writing of this book and chapter. Every experience is a doorway to multiplicities (Nicolaides, 2008); if we learn how to receive them, the potential is limitless. Limitless potentialities are the stuff of transformation. The stuff of experience is in the intra-actions that are felt through the practice of *In-scending*, beneath the story, to (un)story them, to vitalize multiple potentials. When we practice *In-scending* beneath a story of an experience, a portal opens for multiple unexpected sensations that make new things, making space for *Awaring* new meanings. When we tell the story as we want it to be—that is, to tell a tale of experience—the new things also come, but differently, in that they are still stuck in a particular telling, a particular frame. *In-scending* activates an (un) story so that the vital content of experience makes something new: a story not to be erased.

A word about the method. Following the phenomenon in Martha's storytelling, I am able to further theorize and name the contours of a nomadic theory of adult learning. In the following, I practice *In-scending* as a method of embodied reflexivity (e.g., Vettraino et al., 2019) enacted through a combination of reflexive writing and methodical investigation of photographs stored in albums, newspaper and magazine articles, official correspondence, and other such personal archives (Kuhn, 2002; Luttrell, 2010; Somerville, 2004). Telling stories from memory is not mere nostalgia or sentimental reminiscence, but an interpretative, political, and creative engagement that asks us to question: What does it mean to be human? How do we know? Who can be a knower? What is knowledge? (Hendry, 2011).

This theorizing is complemented by that of methodologists who maintain that "qualitative approaches are thought to be more concerned with what it means to be human—or ontological concerns" (Gilgun, 2002; cited in Piercy & Benson, 2005, p. 108). This methodological approach elicits a deeper comprehension of humans' experiences—i.e., the experiences of multiple types of human beings—as affected by the embodied dimensions of race, sexuality, dis/ability, class, gender, im/migration status, war, violence, abuse, displacement, and so on. Reflexivity is both a concept and a process intended to elucidate a researcher's imbrication and investments in an inquiry (e.g., Alvesson & Sköldberg, 2017; Hesse-Biber, 2007). This practice echoes the movement of *In-scending*, inquiring beneath the experience of experience, intra-actively engaging with the remembrance of stories and the documented story that my mother tells over and over again.

The practice of reflexivity involves a researcher's explicit and introspective analysis of her relationship to social constructs such as minority, feminine, violence, as relevant to the research inquiry and/or the social world in which she is enacting that inquiry. Reflexivity, then, "must be seen as a dialogue—challenging perspectives and assumptions both about the social world and of the researcher him/herself" (Palaganas et al., 2017, p. 427). A researcher's positionality pairs with the particularities of her discursive and material body; therefore, an embodied approach to reflexivity requires that the researcher attune to her body in the present moment. Embodied reflexivity "is about being wholly conscious of one's own feelings and emotions in order to be fully immersed in the here and now" (Vettraino et al., 2019, pp. 219–220).

In-scending is such a practice of embodied reflexivity, working with the material of my mother's telling and re-telling of her experience of the Six-Day War and how it served to both tether and make sense of the trauma of her displacement. Her life twisted and turned in unimaginable ways, pulling at the tether to keep her connected to her place of belonging while becoming someone new. I perform this method by practicing *In-scending* into the material of Martha's life found in photographs, magazine articles, newspaper writing, and official correspondence during a period of living in Singapore. I engage this practice to (un)story the telling of a story that anchors my mother's life so that it may uncover potential that I was not attuned to as her daughter. Freedom is one aim of generative knowing. Freedom signals creation and permission to make something different. To make something different frees us from the system's desire to keep reproducing the same thing, its dominance. Freedom is vitality. Vitality is potential that creates something new, different, joyful.

At the beginning of my research on learning and ambiguity, *communion* was one way I described a doorway that connects us to the unknown possibilities that lie waiting beneath the experience of experience. I selected communion as a way to signify that adult learning may take shape with someone or something that is marked by intimacy, vulnerability, and (co)union in the intra-actions of self and all (Nicolaides, 2008, 2015). I have evolved my definition to attune to the intimacy of what I found as I furthered my research; *In-scending* more closely conveys an aspect of generative knowing that requires vulnerability and intimacy with the not-foreknown. *In-scending* is a practice of inquiry as embodied reflexivity, reflecting the partiality and limitations of one's capacity to know reality without the sensations of the experience. The invisible world of experience, its veiled side, is a space of vital potentials all-ready and not-yet, a more vital side of learning that does not respond well as an instrument of (re)production. Reality is a liquid thing (Nicolaides & Marsick, 2016), like stepping into water that at first feels separate to the skin, and then as we *In-scend* deeper into the water, that water taking us in, we become skin-water. *In-scending* is not without grief, loss, and rejection, but it is also not without sweetness. *In-scending* into the deep, beneath the unknown, demands the surrender of armor, defenses against the mystery of what is becoming. *In-scending* evokes a sweetness that comes from receiving sensations from beneath experience. I practice *In-scending* beneath the glossy magazine articles, beneath the stories, and stones, where Martha is not a single story that can be erased.

The period of life that I am recollecting lies along a temporal arc that begins with the Six-Day War in June of 1967, but is concentrated in the years between 1982 and 2000 when Martha lived in Singapore. *Awaring* connotes the meaning that emerges from the not fore-known, an aspect of generative knowing that arises from spaces of possibility that *In-scending* lets you find. *Awaring* captures the making-meaning of the vital potential all-ready and not-yet that emerged through Martha's storytelling: *life is already written; imagination makes happenings*. In what follows I offer bits of talk, writing, and recollection that come from the various sources I described above. These writings are intra-active acts with the material that (un)story Martha, making stones speak in the deep waters that flow between the intra-active engagements that make mother and daughter. Generative knowing makes something new, a story not to be erased.

Life Is Already Written

We were not ready for the Six-Day War. We were living in Jerusalem in the suburb of Beit Hanina. We had moved from Nablus to Jerusalem as my father opened up three pharmacies around Ramallah, Jerusalem, and Jericho. Our house was across the street from what was known as the Palace of the King. There were Jordanian soldiers who surrounded the villa. The neighborhood was mostly Asia-Minor-Greek and Arab Christians like us, Palestinians, and some embassy families that lived nearby. People were saying that the war was about to begin. Some families thought that it was going to be Jordanian soldiers coming in tanks as victors. The winners were the Israelis. Some families died in our neighborhood. Nassar's vision of pan-Arabism that the Syrian and Jordanian leaders reluctantly went along with was not a very cohesive idea at all. The idea of a coalition made up of unified Arab states that would attack Israel and re-establish the balance of power was a shallow promise. Little did they know that the Israelis would preemptively strike the Egyptian air force on June 5, 1967, and eviscerate them. When we heard the noises of war around us, we retreated to our cellar. (Most houses had them.) When we came out of the cellar a day later, what I saw was devastation. Our house was not the same, our garden was filled with dead or dying soldiers, black from napalm that was used by the Israeli soldiers to eliminate the Jordanian forces in Jerusalem. My father, a pharmacist, immediately went into action with neighbors who were doctors and began to treat soldiers and/or move dead bodies into his Rambler to take them away. The soldiers were all black, dead; some others were barely alive. Our house had no electricity or water, nor did we have access to food. My father was Palestinian born in Jerusalem, we could not move from the house. Our neighbors, some UN people, some embassy people, brought us food and water in abundance. I remember that there was death and destruction all around us, and yet we were surrounded by kindness and generosity. The morning after the sixth day somebody knocked on the door. I opened the door and I saw in front of me an Israeli soldier, a captain. We all spoke English and he said, I am Doctor Batisha's son and a friend of your father. Apparently, Dr. Batisha was a Jewish Greek man who went to university with my father. It was a day after the war ended, and this Jewish Greek man brought my father baskets of food and provisions. The next day more Israeli soldiers came knocking, only this time to confiscate my father's car and all the neighbors' cars to use them as transport vehicles for dead soldiers. We were lucky that we had Greeks of the diaspora 'papers' in addition to Jordanian passports, so the soldiers did not make us leave our house even though we were Palestinians; they put a curfew on us. We lost everything and we were lucky. (Interview, 2020)

Life is already written; fatalism alone leaves something generative behind. Martha's memory of her experience of the Six-Day War is coded by what is sayable and what is not, depending on her audience. A telling of the story that does not dare to go beneath the experience of a reality that is true and (un)believable. She says, "We were not ready," as if war were something to become ready for, to anticipate, to know will happen. What becomes from something not anticipated yet undergone is part of the dynamics of learning that I am describing as generative knowing. "Life is already written" may be the language of what is being and becoming by undergoing it. Written not in stone, not as one narrative, written as a story that you tell and tells-you over and over again, the same and different every time. The Six-Day War, as Martha tells it, was not invited; it was imposed, an experience of life already written. "We lost everything and we were lucky" is the refrain of generativity. Undergoing the experience of loss while at the same time receiving the spontaneous generosity that made living possible for Martha's family is an illustration of this force of knowing. Martha has told the story of the Six-Day War many times over the course of her life, memorialized in articles, newspaper cuttings, correspondence, and interviews. Each time she tells it a little differently. I wonder why that is so. What does this different telling make?

In the following excerpts, I listen to her tell the story of the 1967 Six-Day War to interviewers she spoke with over the course of the 20 years she lived in Singapore, as well as from an interview I conducted with her in January 2020, just before the pandemic made things different for all of us. Martha arrived in Singapore in 1979 with her three children to join Ari, my father, to begin what was supposed to be a two-year assignment . . . and that turned into 20. Not too long after my mother settled into raising her children, myself included, and it became real that we were not moving somewhere else, Martha began to root down into the monsoon-soaked landscape of a rising Singapore under the direction of its Prime Minister, Lee Kwan Yew. In my reading of piles of these artifacts, I was taken by the story of her experience of the Six-Day War that she tells and re-tells, a bedrock of her being that I had not noticed before. Until then I had not noticed that the story of the Six-Day War protected my mother as much as it defined her. I remember, in my late teenage daughter years, when these articles began to proliferate, that I was judgmental of the attention my mother received, annoyed that her life was more vibrant than my own at that time. Returning to the articles, I notice how

A Single Story is a Dangerous Narrative

Martha's storytelling of her experience of the Six-Day War anchors her to her home, a desperate belonging that only now I can relate to as her daughter, in that I, too, long to belong, something marked by an unnatural stillness that has now come undone. I have been curious about my own longing to belong. A sensation I cannot shake is something I wrote about earlier in this book. Reading bits of storytelling recorded in articles about Martha that feature the Six-Day War lets emerge a new way of knowing of my own longing for belonging. In what follows I follow the story of the Six-Day War in my mother's telling to re-story the experience of displacement that altered my mother's life and my own.

Figure 5.4. Martha Featured in Singapore-Based Magazines and Newspapers

----

Martha's Story Written in Magazines about Her Charitable Works Makes Displacement Different

Born in Jordan, Mrs. Nicolaides experienced war when she was only 18 years old. "On June 6th, 1967, I was drinking coffee with my mother on the balcony of our house in Jerusalem when suddenly, there was a siren and announcement that the war had begun," Mrs. Nicolaides remembers. "It was a total shock and it was only one day after I had arrived from Paris where I was studying." But the experience of war reinforced in her the spirit of giving and helping others whenever she could.

(The Art of Giving, by Low Yit Leng, *Singapore Tatler*, December 1990)

Thirteen years into living in Singapore, and she is seen as a "socialite." Socialite refers not so much to a sociable person as to one who is socially prominent, which Martha, a 13-year resident of Singapore, undoubtedly is. A regular face on the society pages of local lifestyle magazines for some time now, the expatriate wife knows many and is known to many among the rich and famous here. But she points out, "I am well known in social circles because of my work in charities. The public functions that I attend are usually related to charity." Martha is a member of every other fund-raising committee in town, in aid of causes ranging from the National Kidney Foundation to the Singapore Dance Theater to LaSalle College. Can a person who is not Mother Theresa care so much, and for people who have nothing to do with her existence? The Jordanian born Martha points to her background. "I was brought up in the midst of war. I witnessed the Six-days war in 1967, and saw people lose their homes, everything. My family was privileged in that our losses were manageable, unlike others who became refugees and homeless instantly."

(In Person, by Chua Bee Hua, The Social Scientist, *Hot Magazine*, Singapore, March 1992)

Although Martha loves beautiful things, she has managed to detach herself from them. "This is easy if you have seen death and suffering," she said. She was living in Jerusalem during the terrible days of the 1967 6-day war. It made her realize that there are more important things in life than mere possessions.

(Renaissance Lady, by Kelly Chopard, *Home & Decor*, 1995)

In 1995, living in Singapore, I was giving a talk about Palestine, my experience of the Six-Day War in Palestine and the ongoing conflict with Israel. I had a petit mal while I was giving the talk. Later that evening, when you and I were having dinner, you noticed that the left side of my face was drooping. I remember you were frantic to figure out what was wrong, your father away on a trip, your then-husband away working in Indonesia. A week later I was flown to [the] Mayo Clinic and there I stayed for a month for observation and a brain biopsy. The doctor thought I had a brain tumor and so they went into my brain. The doctor thought I would have 6 weeks to live. I remember your sister Katia, your father and brother all crying and I was very calm. What is written is written.

(Petit Mal, Interview, January 2020)

I used to believe that there is only one story, one narrative, of my mother's experience of the Six-Day War, until I began to recognize its oppression. One narrative is a dangerous thing: a line from a metissage I constructed a short time ago. The story of Martha living through the Six-Day War was told and retold as a foundational stone of her displacement, making it something different: a novelty, not a trauma. The practice of *In-scending* doesn't become something immediately; it implies a kind of "groping experimentation and its layout resorts to measures that are not very respectable, rational, or reasonable" (Deleuze & Guattari, 1994). Thinking does not reproduce the same thing; it becomes something else, reviving it. In this way, generative knowing is not a problem of science, which seeks reference points and conditions of certainty. Generative knowing is practiced through deep inquiry. *In-scending* is one form of deep inquiry in that it follows the intra-active entanglements of the sensation encountered beneath the experience of experience. Drawing on Deleuze and Guattari, they describe affect as a "preconscious ... pre-individual" force, "not an action but a capacity for activation" (Ticineto Clough, 2009, p. 48), that extends beyond human perception and intention. *In-scending* is such a force, a deep practice of inquiry that creates generative knowing as affect. The sensation of displacement is an affect not easy to hold. Erasing the displacement and telling it like a story, the Six-Day War, makes it something different. In my mother's case, an experience in the past, novel in that it gives her cover to act in the center of a community that is not her own. I had not thought about the power in my mother's narrative of the Six-Day War as a way to become real in a land so far away from home. Potential that touched many people's lives in those days of Singapore's city-state making.

Imagination Makes Happenings—Loss-And-Start-Over-Again

I wanted to go to a free country after surviving the Six-Day War in 1967. I was engaged to be married to my high school sweetheart, who was living in Beirut (*a marriage that did not happen because soon after I arrived in Beirut I left my fiancé, who was not faithful to me during the time we were living apart*). I decided that I would travel to Beirut to visit him. Our families had agreed it would be best for me to leave Jerusalem, given the precarious conditions of the post-war that was our family's reality. Another loss-and-start-over-again was beginning. It was after the 1967 Six-Day War when my family decided that it would be best for me to go to Beirut and join my fiancé. At the airport, an Israeli officer took my passport, the Jordanian passport, and Greek Diaspora papers and put a big Israel stamp on them. I remember that he smiled and told me, "You can never return." I have not been home to Palestine since 1967.

It was many months after I had left Beirut to join my parents in Aman, Jordan, when I received a call from your father. I liked his voice. His sister and my uncles had arranged for us to meet via phone and correspondence, as your father was in the United States completing his studies. It was thought that he and I would make a good match. I was heartbroken and wanted to go to a freer country. I agreed to accept his marriage proposal after several calls and letters. Though I yearned to further my education, it was after the war, and money was a scarce resource, so I took the offer to go to a freer country where there were no wars. I married your father. I am a survivor.

Thank God your father was sent to Greece for work, and there we stayed before moving to Singapore. I swore that my girls will be strong, and I gave them complete freedom to explore and become women. Gave you, both, a conscience. I gave you a lot of love. I made mistakes. I am not sorry for those mistakes, because every time I made those mistakes, it was for a reason, to save something.

No love, No life. You lose people that you love. There is strength in accepting whatever comes. Yiany, my brother, died when I was 7 years old. I remember my mother wearing a black kimono with flowers. I went to hold her hand and she said, "It's ok, he's going to be with the angels." Very strong, my mother. There was a kind of acceptance by all the women in my family, with what they lost. They lost everything so many times.

Loss-and-start-over-again was our family legacy.

We loved harder and laughed louder, as loss and death were common experiences. My mother was 28 years old when my father died. Soon after she remarried. In those days a widow was easy prey, and the children needed protection. I was surrounded by love. I am a strong woman, and I love to give love to everybody. I try to understand people, I try to love people, I don't hate anybody. Jane [pseudonym] was an orphan at our school. One of my friends, Tina [pseudonym], was from a wealthy family, and one day as we were leaving school to go back home for the weekend, she asked me why I was hanging out with Jane, whose mother was said to be a woman of ill repute and that it was rumored that she slept with a priest. I remember my great grandmother, Katerina, heard about the conversation and was furious with Tina. She called me to her house and told me that "we do not agree to such things, Marthoula, tell me about Jane." I told her Jane and her mother lived in the monastery attached to our school in one room that was divided by a curtain where she and her mother live, sleep and eat. Katerina, my great grandmother, was aghast, and said we do not accept this. She filled a basket with food, clothing, all kinds of things, and asked me to take it to Jane. I told her that she would be upset, but my great grandmother insisted. Jane and I became good friends, and we would study together. She told me the last time we spoke, "Marthoula, I will never forget you and your family, you were the kindest people in my life."

The women in our family are filled with love, kindness, humor, and generosity. Generosity is part of our lineage.

The nuns taught me to love everyone. They were of the Jewish faith converted to Catholicism and embraced all people of faith. I instilled that in you and your siblings. Sr. Joel was from Turkey and has the gift of palm reading. She looked at my palm and said, "Marthoula you're a strong woman. You are not going to get married in Jordan. You're going to go overseas, but when you go abroad, you are going to leave an impact wherever you go." I was 16 years old when she read that on my palm. I laughed and she said, "Don't laugh, it is what I see." Mother Eta was an Irish nun and very strict. She said, "You know, I see you one day, Marthoula, becoming quite a big personality somewhere in the world." And it happened. In Greece, we led a wonderful life surrounded by love and family. When we moved to Singapore in 1979, I became very good friends with the first Singaporean families: Chinese Singaporeans, Indian Singaporeans, Malaysian Singaporeans, and the international community that had begun to gather there. I grew up in Singapore. I was 33 years old when we moved there, with the three of you. I became very active in a lot of charities. Your father and I helped to establish the Singapore Opera and the Singapore Ballet. We were part of the group that started both in Singapore in the early 80s. (Interview, 2020)

What Generative Knowing Makes

Mother-daughter relationships are complex, a cliché that holds true. When the pandemic forced my parents and me to live in a lockdown state as an inter-generational family, I was not prepared for the daily reminders of aging parents. The commitment to accompany my parents as they live the final third of their lives was now something different. Experiencing the lockdown life that COVID imposed on us *Ruptured* the vision we had all agreed to, to walk alongside. What began as a comfortable arrangement of walking along became an experience of keeping healthy and alive. It was not lost upon me that I was living in a state of anxiety and fear of getting COVID-19 that would kill my parents—a state of war I had not experienced before. The very experience of displacement I was discovering in my mother's story (and my father's, the subject of the next chapter) was now my own. A global pandemic had rendered us lucky, trapped in our shared home, prisoners of an invisible force. Writing this book under the shroud of the pandemic was an unexpected catalyst to working with the material that life presented me. The experience of living through a global pandemic, an experience I could not fore-know. Generative knowing was a way for me to encounter the multiple *Ruptures* in my knowing, daily. Who is my mother? Who is my father? Who am I now? In this pressured lockdown reality, where nothing remained hidden, the practice of *In-scending* made way for the stories that I had known to become real. The stories that were living in the past come to the foreground of the now, to live me, to (un)story my story, opening me up to receive a different potential for being and becoming. I knew Martha as a beautiful, gracious, loving, joyful, courageous woman, but I did not know her as a displaced woman who experienced the trauma of war, and who had to leave behind a self she knew to become someone different. A woman who encountered an unexpected life, and a woman who created a life unexpectedly. Her story is my story. Her people are my people: Asia-Minor-Greek-Palestinian-Christians courageously telling their story, not being erased. Not erased is the creative potential of Martha's story of the Six-Day War.

Generative knowing begins a new story for my mother and me to live into. We live together in a conscious accompaniment to the end of life. I am becoming a daughter who wants to know my mother differently as we intersect physically, cooking in the kitchen together, our souls reterritorializing the stuff of our stories not to be erased. Stories that liberate and heal the lineage of women who came before us and who will come after us.

Notes:

1. Metissage, or braiding, of cultural forms through the simultaneous revalorization of oral traditions and reevaluation of Western concepts has led to the recovery of occulted histories. In the effort to recover their unrecorded past, contemporary writers and critics have come to the realization that opacity and obscurity are necessarily the precious ingredients of all authentic communication: "il est au fond de toute parole... la matière obscure d'un informule." Since history and memory have to be reclaimed either in the absence of hard copy or in full acknowledgment of the

ideological distortions that have colored whatever written documents and archival materials do exist, contemporary women writers especially have been interested in reappropriating the past so as to transform our understanding of ourselves. Their voices echo the submerged or repressed values of our cultures. They rewrite the "feminine" by showing the arbitrary nature of the images and values which Western culture constructs, distorts, and encodes as inferior by feminizing them.

2. Palestine is complex. I recommend you read Nur Masalha's *Palestine: A Four Thousand Year History* (2018) to become better acquainted with this complexity. It might be helpful to the reader to know that the concept of Palestine has multiple beginnings. Masalha articulates the following, which I find useful for those who are not aware of the complexity that is Palestine. "The history of Palestine, unlike the myth-narratives of the Old Testament, has multiple 'beginnings' into a geo-political concept and a distinct territorial polity. The concept of Palestine is often approached in an abstract or ahistorical way, rather than as a contextualized representation of an entity whose (physical, administrative, territorial and cultural) boundaries have evolved and changed across three millennia. But there are no pure ideas or an ideal concept of Palestine per se; empirical evidence and human experience are fundamental to the formation of ideas and knowledge about Palestine. Crucially, we do not know Palestine only 'from without' through perceptions and generalizations but also 'from within' through embodied experiences and affectations . . . there are multiple beginnings and multiple meanings to the idea of Palestine, where the idea came from, how the identity of the ideal of Palestine, evolved and was experienced through and across time (Khronos & Kairos) . . . To borrow from Heidegger's notion of being and time (2010) and temporality (past, present, and future) and the way human beings experience the world through time, ideas, terms and discourses on Palestine should be explored synchronically and diachronically as well as the human experiences of Palestine time . . . terms and concepts evolve multi-linearly and discursively and are experienced differently by different people" (pp. 8–9).

3. Sayigh, Rosemary. (2004). "Survivors of the 1948 expulsions: A second call for a race against time." In Dua' Nakhala, Muna El-Tamemy, & Helda Kojstek (Eds.), *Between the archival forest and the anecdotal trees: A multidisciplinary approach to Palestinian social history*. Birzeit University, Palestine.

4. Lee Kuan Yew served as Prime Minister of Singapore from 1959 to 1990. He is widely recognized as the national founding father.

References

Alvesson, M., & Sköldberg, K. (2017). *Reflexive methodology: New vistas for qualitative research.* sage.

Daloz, L. A. P. (1997). *Common fire: Leading lives of commitment in a complex world.* Beacon Press.

Deleuze, G., & Guattari, F. (1994). *What is philosophy?* (H. Tomlinson & G. Burchell, Trans.). Columbia University Press. (Original work published 1991)

Dewey, J. (1929). *The quest for certainty: A study of the relation of knowledge and action*. Minton, Balch.

Dewey, J. (1934). *Art as experience*. Penguin.

Dewey, J. (1938). *Logic: The theory of inquiry*. Henry Holt.

Gay, R. (2014). *Bad feminist: Essays*. HarperCollins.

Hendry, P. (2011). *Engendering curriculum history*. Routledge.

Hesse-Biber, S. N. (2007). Handbook of Feminist Research. Sage Publications.

Hoggan, C. D. (2016). Transformative learning as a metatheory: Definition, criteria, and typology. *Adult Education Quarterly, 66*(1), 57–75. https://doi.org/10.1177/0741713615611216

Kuhn, A. (2002). *Family secrets: Acts of memory and imagination*. Verso.

Lorde, A. (2020). *The selected works of Audre Lorde*. Norton.

Luttrell, W. (2010). "A camera is a big responsibility": A lens for analysing children's visual voices. *Visual Studies, 25*(3), 224–237. https://doi.org/10.1080/1472586X.2010.523274

Masalha, Nur. (2018). *Palestine: A four thousand year history*. Zed Books.

Mezirow, J. (2000). *Learning as transformation: Critical perspectives on a theory in progress*. Wiley.

Nicolaides, A. (2008). *Learning their way through ambiguity: Explorations of how nine developmentally mature adults make sense of ambiguity*. EdD dissertation, Teachers College, Columbia University.

Nicolaides, A. (2015). Generative learning: Adults learning within ambiguity. *Adult Education Quarterly, 65*(3), 179–195.

Nicolaides, A., & Marsick, V. J. (2016). Understanding adult learning in the midst of complex social "liquid modernity." *New Directions for Adult and Continuing Education 2016* (149), 9–20.

Palaganas, E. C., Sanchez, M. C., Molintas, V. P., & Caricativo, R. D. (2017). Reflexivity in qualitative research: A journey of learning. *Qualitative Report, 22*(2). http://nsuworks.nova.edu/tqr/vol22/iss2/5

Piercy, F. P., & Benson, K. (2005). Aesthetic forms of data representation in qualitative family therapy research. *Journal of Marital and Family Therapy, 31*(1), 107–119. https://doi.org/10.1111/j.1752-0606.2005.tb01547.x

Sayigh, Rosemary. (2004). Survivors of the 1948 expulsions: A second call for a race against time. In Dua' Nakhala, Muna El-Tamemy, & Helda Kojstek (Eds.), *Between the archival forest and the anecdotal trees: A multidisciplinary approach to Palestinian social history*. Birzeit University, Palestine.

Somerville, M. (2004). Tracing bodylines: The body in feminist poststructural research. *International Journal of Qualitative Studies in Education, 17*(1), 47–65. https://doi.org/10.1080/0951839032000150220

Ticineto Clough, P. (2009). The new empiricism: Affect and sociological method. *European Journal of Social Theory, 12*(1), 43–61. https://doi.org/10.1177/1368431008099643

Vettraino, E., Linds, W., & Downie, H. (2019). Embodied reflexivity: Discerning ethical practice through the Six-Part Story Method. *Reflective Practice, 20*(2), 218–233. https://doi.org/10.1080/14623943.2019.1575197

SIX

 Mother Nature: Signals from a Different Plane

A RI USED METAPHOR TO DESCRIBE the long span of this life, with all its phases spanning World War II, the Nabka, the Six-Day War,[1] the eventual migration to the United States, and global professional life. On our way to his first appointment with the "red devil" (what we called chemotherapy when he was being treated for his non-Hodgkin's lymphoma), he asked me to stop the car and turned to speak this metaphor that has never left me: *I feel like a mangrove tree with roots in the air seeking and thirsty for home.* Ari is a displaced person, displaced from his original home, family, community, church, and friends due to geopolitical power moves not of his own making. The 1998 U.N. Commission on Human Rights[2] defines displaced people as "persons or groups of persons who have been forced or obliged to flee or leave their homes or places of habitual residence, in particular as a result of or in order to avoid the effects of armed conflict, situations of generalized violence, violations of human rights, or natural or human-made disasters and who have not crossed an internationally recognized state border." This was the context that Ari was embedded in as his life unfolded from the date of his birth in September 1931 until he was forced to emigrate to the United States in the mid-1950s, and his professional life took him around the globe more times than can be counted. He is now 90 years old and lives with my mother and me in a multi-generational home, where there is earth more like clay than fertile ground, yet it receives Ari's planting. His roots, still thirsty, have found ground, still longing for home.

In January 2020, I interviewed Ari as a way to listen into the story of his experience of the trauma of becoming a displaced person. As a phenomenologist (in the way I take up this philosophically-drenched methodology), I listened for the voices of his experience by following the stories that Ari chose to tell in the way he wanted to tell them. To tell his story he drew a timeline from the first day he could remember to now, and walked me through each significant moment that punctuated the lifeline. He gave voice to remembered experiences, and he used old black-and-white pictures from albums that somehow were carried through the *Ruptures* of displacement, kept like keepsakes of a life taken, and proof of home. The lifeline, punctuated with dates and names of events, photos, and accompanied storytelling, allowed me to listen into the invisible world of his life. I listened to hear what got stirred in me, what reconstituted my own knowing of Ari, and the relational being and becoming that we were living into together in his elder years. I follow the signals of his life unfolding in unexpected and unknown ways of seeing and hearing. Ari gave a name to the power that moved him through various displacements: *mother nature*. The vitality he used to describe mother nature grabbed my attention as a way that Ari found to learn beyond fear and receive a life unexpected. Ari's life experiences are evocative of generative knowing: ways of being and becoming that activate potential creatively. Unexpectedly, out of displacement Ari creates a surprising life that gives generously the gifts of love, family, adventure, and eventually a ground to belong to. I will put sound to pictures and his living as an illustration of how in the intra-activeness of our relatedness generative knowing emerges to activate potential that is all-ready for each of us to uncover. Ten years ago, when Ari turned 80, my siblings and I began to inquire: what would be a way to respond to our aging parents that would make the biggest space for them to thrive until their end of life? Year after year we turned and re-turned this inquiry until it became clear to us all that the best choice was for my parents to join me in a temperate climate, affordable, a college town where we could live together and I would take the lead in accompanying my parents to their end of life from near and my siblings and their families from afar. It sounds like a noble decision, one that took almost ten years to make for all of us. In January 2019, my parents moved to Athens, Georgia, in the United States, an irony that is not lost upon us as Greek-Palestinians who spent many years in Athens, Greece—a kind of return to home. In February 2020, the global pandemic turned this noble act of accompaniment into lockdown. At the same time, I was beginning to put together the outline of this book and use my research leave that semester to write it. The pandemic turned everything upside down. My research leave was more of a dance with COVID-19 avoidance and protecting my parents from infection than a leave to focus on one thing: the writing of my book. There is luminosity in the dark; the mystery that generative knowing uncovers became a way to be in relationship with COVID-19, a lockdown reality with my immune-compromised parents, and a research leave, that left me. I turned to the everyday lived experience of a global pandemic at home with my parents in lockdown as data for my book. Every day was a *Rupture* of known reality and response-ability. The fluid ontology *Ruptured*, wide open with nowhere to hide, escape to, or avoid. This real experience demanded attention. So I turned downward into the dark mystery of experience, lived and living, that became the content of uncovering the power and aspects of generative knowing. After all, the doorway to generative knowing was ambiguity, where I began my research years ago. Ambiguity marked every aspect of pandemic life. So I *In-scended* into the daily sensations, open to what emerged. What comes in this chapter is the intra-active ontology of generational trauma, that of displacement that my father and I both experienced, yet felt differently about across different temporalities. Mother nature has ways of making life felt in the roughness of living, as she did with Ari and me.

Before I go any further, there is a shadow part to Ari's surprisingly potent life. He also comes from ground layered with four centuries of colonial power (at least in the space of my family's lineage)—from the Byzantines to the Ottoman, to the British Mandate, and then the formation of Israel. My people, my father's people, moved with the tides of power that pushed indigenous people out to make way for the dominant power's self-interests. Mutual interests are forgotten as the power of self-interest (I use "self" here to connote both self and society) privileged their power. My father has never forgotten the forced power over his life, his home taken, and his lifeline interrupted, and it was a sore point in our family. This single-pointed hurt—displaced from home—framed every conversion my father engaged with, be it casual or professional, in the context of family, friends, acquaintances, and unplanned encounters. His refrain was the catastrophe that the British Mandate caused his family and the formation of the State of Israel that did not consider Palestine and the Palestinians who were already there. This is where the conversation gets tricky. Zionism declared that Palestine was an empty space waiting for Israel to become.

Growing up, we were well trained to tense up and cringe when my father raised the issue of Palestine and the royal catastrophe that the British Mandate befell upon his people—Christian Palestinians, Muslims, and people of the Jewish faith (distinct from Zionist, lest you think he is antisemitic, which is a very blurry boundary, since he and I are both Semites given our cultural and ethnic heritage). Under the Ottoman Empire, my father remembers peace and prosperity for all of his people as long as the laws of the land under Ottoman rule were respected. It was a compromise and mutual contract that lasted 400 years. And then the British Mandate came. Under the British Mandate my father remembers deceit, trickery, and betrayal, and the paradoxical truth, that his father was employed by the British Mandate office for a while, and supported his family in the way to which they were accustomed. Palestine provides fertile ground for paradox, complexity, contradictions, multiple truths, and sufferings. There is no clear line that can tell the story of Palestine. There are entangled roots that tell many stories of suffering and survival that continue today, long after my father had to leave his home and was lucky to create a new life for his family. "Lucky" is a source of power for displaced people. Lucky to survive, lucky to start again, lucky to outlast the many almost-fatal encounters with death that Ari's story will tell.

When the conversation took a turn to Palestine, our bodies were trained to tighten because, how dare we, Asia-Minor-Greek-Palestinians, have a voice that differed from the rest of the world, who saw that the only great catastrophe was Hitler and Nazi Germany's deliberate persecution of approximately six million Jews, five million prisoners of war, Romany, homosexuals, and other victims, including Greeks who sheltered Jews in Greece. In conversation spaces, we knew that anything related to Jews and Israelis would have pride of place, while our father's experience of a different and yet equally real catastrophe did not. That's how we lived around the world, apologetic that we also had a story to tell of persecution and loss that was always silenced, self-censored out of fear, and/or by the looks others would begin to give us when my father's conversation would take the turn toward his Palestinian story. A different story, and yet real. I have always wondered: why is it my father's story, his lived experience of a time in his homeland of Palestine, was not allowable? That he was the one who would get into trouble when the conversation took this turn, as if it were forbidden to tell a different story. To have a different perspective on a reality that was painful for him and fruitful for others. I remember his good childhood friends and my uncles telling Ari to forget those days, that everyone was to blame for the catastrophe that is still Palestine, and that he was lucky to get away and start over again.

As a scholar, I have become interested in the decolonizing movements by scholars such as Ahmed (2017), Stein et al. (2020), Spivak (1988), and

Haraway (2016), to name a few. For my father's story, I borrow from the methods and practices of social cartographies (Stein et al., 2020). Social cartographies can support people to clarify the conditions and particularities of their own context and to sit with and learn from contradictions without seeking to immediately resolve them. Cartographies support the depth and rigor of intellectual processes by orienting these processes through critical generosity, attention to difference, and self-implication, and thus avoid simplistic or universal solutions to complex problems. At the same time, cartographies create space for the breadth and integrity of the affective and relational processes that are involved in facing the full scope of current challenges, and walking (and stumbling) together toward other possibilities, without determining the direction or outcome of change in advance of its doing. Social cartographies can serve as a kind of "decolonial gesture," which is, according to Marboeuf and Yakoub (2019), "conceived of in terms of discomfort, a discomfort that is not ephemeral, but long and shared," and thus "we must learn to stay with problems, to stay with the trouble" (p. 4). Indeed, cartographies invite those who engage them to "stay with the trouble" (Haraway, 2016) rather than turn away in search of immediate relief or resolution. Further, cartographies respect the different pace of each person's learning, while also reminding people in dominant positions that they are accountable to those who are negatively affected by their learning and its pace, particularly given the magnitude and the urgency of the challenges that we face. The intention is ultimately to support people in making and taking responsibility for their own critically informed decisions about how to address pertinent challenges within their situated contexts.

In offering Ari's story and mine, intertwined as they are, such a cartography may prompt the reader to grapple with the fact that generative ways of knowing as ways of being and becoming might be unintelligible to us from within our inherited frames—and that we might be reproducing further harm by assuming that they are (Ahenakew, 2016; Marboeuf & Yakoub, 2019; Spivak, 1988). Some stories tend to feed desires to consume (and, generally, romanticize and/or pathologize) differences, and to relate to others by knowing about them in ways that do not actually interrupt harmful projections, power relations, or dominant frames of reference. Generative knowing attempts to liberate Ari's and my story from the frames that lock meaning in place and fixate truth. Ari's story is also true—true in that he experienced suffering for holding onto his story in a particular way, sometimes more fixed in habituated frames that did not liberate him or the story. Making a social cartography of Ari's story and mine activates different possibilities for decolonizing our stories of displacement, remaking them into a vibrant potential that releases the stories of our people, our lineage, from colonialization, and the reproduction of unjust power.

Decolonizing my father's story is part of the generative movement that emerges in our conversation space. Somehow, his story became mine; somehow, his experiences remain real and true in me; somehow, his reality becomes generative, opening doorways, signals from a different territory, for new potential to emerge. A life 90 years long and deep grows beyond fear and survival into something full and whole.

Mother Nature

I was 3 years old. We were living in the Old City of Jerusalem. Across the street from our house was a Spanish nunnery that ran a daycare. I remember I was crying all the time, looking out the window to find my mother waving her hand from our home across the street. She would be at the window at our house, waving her hand, so I could stop crying. That was a big change for me, and I just couldn't accept that I am not at home. This was the first trauma.

When I was 6 years old, we moved to Katamon, a suburb just outside of Jerusalem. That meant I had to take a bus to school in the Old City and look for excuses to visit my grandmother, who lived in our house in the Old City, so I could also visit my friends who still lived in the Old City.

This was a nice and very peaceful time.

We were very lucky that in that period between the start and finish of World War II we still had peace and prosperity. The war was not affecting us in Palestine . . . until 1945.

Just as World War II was coming to an end, the problems began. Jewish gangs had begun organizing themselves in the 1920s before I was born, as a result of the Balfour Declaration. Their activities were escalating under the conditions of World War II ending and the British

Mother Nature: Signals from a Different Plane

Figure 6.1. Young Aristotle

Mandate also approaching an end. As these two realities were ending, the Middle East region was experiencing other destabilizations. Under these conditions, the Irgun and the Haganah began to terrorize Greek and Arab Palestinian civilians as part of their work to eliminate terrorists and anyone and anything that interfered with their mission, claiming that Palestine is Eretz Israel (Land of the Jews).

Those goons were just blowing up things. At that time I was going to school in the Old City, always afraid of riding the bus or not returning home. There were all kinds of stories in the papers, and news broadcasts that this or that building, or street corner, or piece of land, was bombed or blown up by these gangs. I was afraid that one of these bombs would hit the bus and me in it. The bus company was Arab, and they were forced to cover the buses with steel plates as bullets came from Monte Fiore—A Jewish suburb outside the city walls.

I just lived in fear.

As Greek Palestinians, we lived in a predominantly Arab neighborhood, with some European families in our midst. The Jews chose to build separate communities and live alone, segregated by choice. To signal to our neighbors who we were when making our way back and forth to the Old City, we would wear a Palestinian Keffiyehs (scarf) as a symbol of our belonging to the neighborhood. One day I decided to visit my cousin, who lived a mile or so away from us. I forgot to wear my scarf that day, and a few days before there had been some killings between the Jewish and Arab gangs. This was during the 1945–46 period. As I was walking to my cousin's house, I was attacked by an Arab gang member who held a knife to my neck. I started to curse him in Arabic, and that saved my life. "Oh, you are not Jewish?" he said, and I replied, "No, I am not." We spent some time in conversation about his grief and seeking revenge for his murdered brother before I continued to walk to my cousin's house.

Speaking Arabic saved my life.

Aliki interjects during the interview with a parallel story:

Ari, do you remember when I was in Jerusalem working on my Master's thesis? In 1991 when I was completing my Master's thesis in conflict resolution and peace education studies at The American University in Washington, DC, I went to Palestine to collect data and facilitate a peace education workshop between Israeli and Palestinian youth. While in the Old City, I was walking from my aunt's house near Jaffa Gate to complete some errands in preparation for my workshop. Two young Palestinian men, their heads wrapped in Kaffiyehs, approached me and pushed me into a stone wall that lined the narrow cobblestone streets I was walking along on my way to complete an errand near Damascus Gate. They called me an Israeli Sharmuta (slang for whore) and wanted to know what I was doing walking the Old City cobblestone streets alone. I spoke to them in broken Arabic and fluent Greek, showing them the cross I was wearing around my

Figure 6.2. Aristotle from 1946 to 1948

neck, when an elderly gentleman came walking toward us quickly, waving his cane and speaking in Arabic. The young men lowered their hands from me and greeted the elderly man politely, recognizing him. He scolded them, and they apologized and moved on. The elderly man turned to me and said in Greek, you are Aristotle's daughter. I knew your grandfathers, Theodore Nicolaides and Theodore Ninos. I knew your grandmother, Costandia, and your mother, too. Then he warned me that these are dark days in Jerusalem and that I should be very cautious walking alone. This man, Elias, was a member of the Greek Palestinian community still living in the Old City.

He saved my life.

Ari continues:

The atrocities had started to get more frequent, and bigger bombs were making things difficult. You can read in the history books about the terrorist attacks from the Irgun. One such attack was the bombing of the King David Hotel, which was near our house. In 1946, the Irgun was one of the Jewish gangs trying to gain independence. They disguised themselves as mild delivery persons and placed explosives inside milk jugs in the basement of the King David Hotel, which was also serving as the secretariat of the British Mandate, and blew it up. The debris from that bomb came into our garden and just missed our house.

As Christmas 1947 was approaching, the Jewish gangs blew up the Park Hotel outside Rehavia (Jewish Community) and only yards away from our house. This caused most of our window panes to shatter, making our life unbearable in the winter cold. We locked our house, took a suitcase of clothes, and went to my grandmother's in the Old City of Jerusalem until we could get the house repaired. We were never allowed to return, and we lost it all. The Haganah had occupied that part of the Ktamon suburb near Rehavia, and non-Jews could not be in the suburbs anymore. We never went back.

During that time, the Arabs and the Jews were increasing their acts of terrorism. Jewish gangsters would move into any space that was empty, regardless of who had lived there. This happened to the area where our house was. Some Jewish people managed to move into our house while we were staying with my grandmother in the Old City, a time when we couldn't return to our home, thinking it was not livable due to the bomb's impact.

That was the last time I lived in my house: December 1947.

I left behind all kinds of things that were mine. I was a Boy Scout, and I had all kinds of instruments, bugles, and drums. All that was lost. I had a violin that I was learning to play. That, too, was lost, because we never could return to our home in Katamon. I still have the key to our home's door. We were stuck living from a suitcase in my grandmother's house in the Old City.

So life continued like that, in fear, but that's all we could do. We lived looking over our shoulders at every doorway, at every turn. A ridiculous life.

We had no choice.

1948 marked the end of the British Mandate. The British had been in Palestine since the end of World War I. We expected some problems to arise then. One of the British officers, who was a friend of my father's, told him that the British would never leave Palestine, that they would stay to protect everyone. He told us, "Don't worry. We're going to leave from the main gate, but we're going to come back from the window." Which was not true, because they never came back, and the Israelis managed to create a country that put us—Greek Palestinians—in a vulnerable place, leaving all Arab Palestinians without the protections to exercise their rights to self-determination, as stipulated in the Mandate by the League of Nations.

We lived in fear. I remember that time as being very unpleasant.

The West Bank and East Jerusalem came under the control of King Hussein of Jordan (1946–1950). Of course, the Arab and Jewish gangs were still trying to find ways to occupy the Old City of Jerusalem. So, sometime between 1948 and before 1949, the Jewish gangs managed to camp on the outside wall. Outside the wall of Jerusalem was Israel; on the inside of the wall was the Kingdom of Jordan. So the Jewish gangs wanted to blow up the wall. This wall was built by Suleiman the Magnificent in the 14th century. And the wall seemed impregnable.

Figure 6.3. The Mortar Bombing

What the Jewish gang members did was to place a big bomb to blow up the wall. And inside, the chosen area of the wall was where my school was, College Des Frères, near Damascus Gate.

There was a bomb threat, and the Jordanian government told all of us living in the Old City to leave so that we would not be harmed. It was a scary time. I had a bicycle, so I took it to The Mount of Olives. I took what I thought was necessary to be saved, because we were not even sure that the city or the wall would stay intact. I took pictures, and I have pictures of that to remind me of this catastrophe. It was such a big bomb. The Jordanian Army detonated the bomb, and when it exploded it emitted only black soot that covered the city in black. The Jewish gang didn't destroy the wall. It did make a small hole, which we could see from the dining room of the school. The school closed because of the destructive effect of the defused bomb, so I had to change schools again.

In 1949, before the truce, there was a truce between King Hussein and the Israeli government. Ben Gurion was the prime minister then. The Israelis wanted to occupy the Old City. But they couldn't, because the Arab League was protecting the walls. And so what did the Israelis do? They sent us about 500 mortars in one night.

One mortar hit the wall opposite our house in Jerusalem and scattered little pieces of mortar through our window. We were all sitting there—all nine of us—because some of the cousins were with us, close to the front of our house in the old city, where the window was. We heard this *zzz boom, zzz boom*, and the proximity of it was getting closer all the time. We were afraid. So, you know what we did? We took mattresses, covered our backs with them, and walked downstairs to the underground room that was in the monastery. (We lived in a monastery with my grandmother at that time.)

They were sending one bomb after another and at all times of the day. One time, I heard the *zzz*, and it hit where I was. All these stones came crumbling down on top of me. And I noticed just in time that three or four steps ahead of me was an underground space. So I jumped in there, and that's what saved me.

I think that there is a power, let's call it mother nature, that you have been given a time to live by this power, mother nature. And if you're careful, you survive the time given to you. One of the bombs hit the

Mother Nature: Signals from a Different Plane

dome of the church of the Holy Sepulchre, and this was the most terrible experience.

As I survived those days, my goal became to move into society to survive without being controlled by fear.

I must have had some kind of aura or something that protects me, that gave me all these opportunities to survive these many near-death experiences. Somehow, even though I was afraid, I was never depressed. As I entered society, not knowing where the other dollar was going to come from so I could buy a piece of bread to survive, I found what I needed. When I needed a dollar, it was in my pocket. I call this power mother nature.

Mother nature was my means of survival. You follow the path that mother nature presents, charted by a power you cannot fore-know.

Keeping that formula in my brain, that mother nature protects me, propelled me through some terrible times, but also some really good times, which created my path to survival.

Figure 6.4. Ari Being Young Adult

Aliki interjects during the interview with a parallel story:

Mother nature resonates in me as well.

Do you remember that a year after you and mom left Singapore, I decided to leave Singapore as well, where I was working with Melissa to build our small educational consulting group? I wanted to leave Singapore after Melissa and I were eliminated as finalists for a big youth education grant that the Ministry of Education in Singapore had invited us to submit an application for. I was embarrassed and afraid about how I would survive without an immediate income source, so I sold everything but my Persian carpets and two suitcases of clothing and arrived in San Francisco ready to discern what my next life path would be. The life of a nun or something different?

In the two years I lived in San Francisco I moved places of residence 16 times. Soon after I arrived in the United States, I discovered that even though I was born there and was a citizen, I had no record of working in the country. As a result, I was 31 years old with lots of experience in social entrepreneurial work in Singapore but no evidence that I knew how to work in an organization in the United States, and therefore was not getting hired for any positions. I had a small amount of savings and, of course, was supported by family; but what you may not remember from that time is that San Francisco has a law that you cannot stay as a guest in a rented home for more than 30 days. At the time, Katia and her family were renting and had not yet bought their San Francisco home. So, 30 days into my life in the United States I had to find a new place to live, only I had no credit card, debt, or record of work, and I could not get an apartment to approve of me as a tenant. So I had to find a different solution. I had to ask for help from complete strangers in the Buddhist community of which I was a member, and friends of friends.

Mother nature, as you say, was at every asking, and when I asked with all kinds of conflicting emotions in my heart such as fear, shame, and wonder, everyone I asked—stranger or friend—said yes, stay on my couch, stay in my extra room, house sit while I am traveling . . . and so I had 16 different homes over 2 years with a suitcase of belongings.

Mother Nature: Signals from a Different Plane

Ari continues his story . . . .

The pattern of barely escaping with my life, since I was a young boy at knife's edge, escaping the shards of windows shattering as a bomb lands nearby, losing all that I consider mine as a young Boy Scout, living in fear and surviving with that fear close by, I wonder how it was possible that I followed a path that mother nature had laid out for me.

There are many stories of moments of surprise and generosity from unexpected people, events, situations that have made this a good life. A broken heart over my first love led me to discover another love, and a family is made. And when I worked for a division of General Motors, and all of a sudden they needed somebody who could speak Greek. The Greek Air Force bought a bunch of airplanes that had our engines, and they needed somebody to represent the company I worked for. The company wanted somebody who spoke Greek and came to me as the only Greek-speaking engineer in the company at the time. So they sent me. I said, "Okay, I'll go for a couple of years, but I'm coming back." My then-supervisor says, "Sure." And two years became three, the three became six. And you know why? Because I spoke languages. It was not my engineering skills that pushed me out into the world; it was my languages. After six years in Greece, they asked me to go to Singapore. I don't speak Chinese, I told them. They said, "No, but you know how to do it in your language, so you can find a way." So they figured out that I can find ways to survive, and they sent me to Singapore, where I was with my family for 21 years.

Mother nature arrived unexpectedly: a dollar in my pocket, an opportunity I had not sought out, a mattress, a way that led me beyond living in fear.

Mother nature is another good name for the *Awaring* aspect that signals generative knowing: ways of being and becoming. Mother nature is Ari's name for the potential that was activated creatively in times he thought he might not survive. Mother nature is a vital energy that Ari receives as he remains faithful and moves through the sensations of fear that haunt him. Looking at a selection of photographs that accompanied the telling of Ari's experience during those years of his life reveals a portrait of the complexity of a known life with boy scout meetings, Easter celebrations, and family gatherings juxtaposed with bombings and near-death experiences. These photos and our stories reveal the vitality of life captured beneath the trauma of displacement. Sensing the signals of mother nature was a language of generative knowing that my father could hear. Learning to recognize and receive those signals is an aspect of generative knowing that I have described as *Awaring*. *Awaring* is different from learning that is acquired; it is learning that is received and not-foreknown. Ari marvels at how many times the force of mother nature arrives unexpectedly as he tells the story of his life. The surprise is the signal Ari senses, *Awaring*, that potential is all-ready.

As I placed the photographs in an asymmetrical timeline with the images of Ari's life between 1941 and 1952, you see mother nature in motion. Images of visiting the zoo; a walk through the ruins of Jericho; a trip to Cairo; a museum visit; a family portrait in the Katamon home garden in the middle of blooming hydrangeas; a picnic one afternoon in Gethsemane together with images of displacement; a portrait of mother and grandmother and Ari in the courtyard of St. Euthymios the first time as refugees; visiting the Church of the Holy Sepulchre after the mortar bombing in 1949; watching the melting of lead and wood; walking the cobblestone streets of the old city; Ari and his sister arm in arm; a portrait as a boy scout just before the bombing of the King David Hotel; a vanishing image of his father, who tragically dies in a car accident after they are displaced; graduation from high school after moving schools every few months due to bombings and curfews, which caused my father to take four more years than usual to complete his high school degree at age 22. Ari's encounters with the persistence of fear and hopeful survival shape 90 years of life. Ari sits now with me and tells me more stories as he tills the clay ground of Athens, Georgia, in the United States, and the potential that new plantings may offer. For Ari, mother nature is the vital energy he continues to sense that is all-ready, moving him through fear and past survival to allow a vitality he recognizes but does not command.

My father is losing his hearing, as do all who make it past the threshold of 90 years of life. I scold him for not wearing his hearing aids regularly so that he does not miss out on any conversations. As I reflect on the ways that my own being and becoming have been intertwined with my father's stories across our lifetimes, I notice that hearing and listening are two different things. Mother nature does not need hearing; she needs listening. Listening to my father's story, I sense a different knowing I cannot command: my father getting closer to ground where life's vitality is all-ready and not yet.

Notes:

1. For deeper insight into the history of Palestine, see Nur Masalha's book *Palestine: A four thousand year history*, first published in 2018 by Zed Books Ltd.
2. https://www.ohchr.org/en/issues/idpersons/pages/issues.aspx

References

Ahenakew, C. (2016). Grafting Indigenous ways of knowing onto non-Indigenous ways of being: The (underestimated) challenges of a decolonial imagination. *International Review of Qualitative Research, 9*(3), 323–340. https://doi.org/10.1525/irqr.2016.9.3.323

Ahmed, S. (2017). *Living a feminist life*. Duke University Press.

Haraway, D. J. (2016). *Staying with the trouble: Making kin in the Chthulucene*. Duke University Press.

Masalha, Nur. (2018). *Palestine: A four thousand year history*. Zed Books.

Marboeuf, O., & Yakoub, J. B. (2019). *Decolonial variations: A conversation between Olivier Marboeuf and Joachim Ben Yakoub*. https://oliviermarboeuf.files.wordpress.com/2019/05/variations_decoloniales_eng_def.pdf

Spivak, G. C. (1988). Can the subaltern speak? In C. Nelson & L. Grossberg (Eds.), *Marxism and the interpretation of culture* (pp. 24–28). Macmillan.

Stein, S., Andreotti, V., Suša, R., Amsler, S., Hunt, D., Ahenakew, C., Jimmy, E., Cajkova, T., Valley, W., Cardoso, C., Siwek, D., Pitaguary, B, D'Emilia, D., Pataxó, U., Calhoun, B., & Okano, H. (2020). Gesturing towards decolonial futures: Reflections on our learnings thus far. *Nordic Journal of Comparative and International Education (NJCIE), 4*(1), 43–65. https://doi.org/10.7577/njcie.3518

SEVEN

 Generative Knowing & the Future of Work[1]

Ahreum Lim

Ahreum Lim is a Ph.D. candidate in Learning, Leadership and Organization Development at University of Georgia. She is interested in intersecting generative knowing theory with the emerging socio-technical complexity in the technocratic culture. In particular, she is interested in researching the human-machine interaction as a phenomenon and developing an effective learning intervention that addresses the human workers' ethical inquiries in face of a different technological entity.

GENERATIVE KNOWING, A NOMADIC THEORY of adult learning, illuminates the path to activating potential in self and society by recognizing their temporal, spatial embodiedness, and acknowledging how they are in the process of being and becoming, particularly in the face of the unknown. What marks the unknown can be understood by its "unusual perplexity" (Dewey, 1910/2007, p. 38). The unknown requires an individual to escape from habits of thought and experiment with new thinking and forms of making meaning. According to generative knowing theory, the departure from the habits of thoughts is only possible through undergoing the experience of experience. Generative knowing's take on experiential learning is different from Kolb's (1984) experiential learning but more aligned with Dewey's (1934) perspective. Generative knowing focuses on the "doing" part of the experience and raises questions such as *What is occurring, what occurred? What is perceived, recognized through such occurrences?* Generative knowing theory brings the "undergoing" part of the experience to light; in other words, it sheds light on the receptivity of individuals to having an experience in experiential learning. Dewey explained doing and undergoing as complementary, reciprocal forces that make up perception, highlighting the importance of undergoing an experience in order to make the experience more esthetic, or educative. In experiential learning, *doing* means an energetic force that enables bare recognition of objects on the basis of established meaning schemes or rules. On the other hand, *undergoing* means a receptive phase of experience that allows one to form a new picture or new schemes.

Undergoing an experience means the growth of experience by deeply engaging oneself in the flow of experience, which requires both sensation and curiosity. The balance of old and new, of far and close, and of strange and familiar is what makes it possible for adult learners to reflect and deeply engage with the unknown; otherwise, they will lose their energy or vitality to be in the space of inquiry. That is, "too much that is easy gives no ground for inquiry; too much of the hard renders inquiry hopeless" (Dewey, 1910/2007, p. 105).

In this chapter, I would like to share my experiences of being receptive in the space of inquiry toward the future of work or, simply put, undergoing the future of work context. Undergoing the future of work sounds ironic, as the future of work embodies the not-yet-actualized context that is only possible through imagination. The "future" of work literally signifies its composite nature of imaginings around changes that are yet to come, coupled with images from sci-fi movies and fiction series, rendering it impossible to experience, let alone undergo, the future of work. Nonetheless, deep immersion into the now proliferating critical inquiries around the future of work (i.e., Bridle, 2018; Broussard, 2018; Crawford, 2021; Danaher, 2019; Rosenblat, 2018; Schwab, 2017) provided me with a vicarious experience in which I revisited my assumptions, beliefs, and stance in the face of the not-yet-fully-recognized phenomena. This chapter sums up how my thinking happened to me and how I interweave the pieces and bits of thoughts through leaning into the not foreknown and all-ready that is the future of work.

The territory of this inquiry brought me into close encounters with timelines of experience that intersected with my past and my upbringing. My narrative regarding the future of work—my research experience in a project which develops the human resource development strategy in a response to the introduction of chatbot technology in a mid-sized health care enterprise—and the underlying belief, desire, assumptions that I revisited after the sensations of visceral feelings (Bateson, 1991) that emerged from the experience, will reveal how I am undergoing a slice of a not-yet-realized future of work. By doing so, this chapter shows how generative knowing plays in the future of work context, or in the context of heightened uncertainty and virtuality.

Doing: Working on a Chatbot Development Project

When I was a research graduate assistant as a master's student in the Workforce Development and Vocational Education Program in South Korea, I was involved in a project to craft a human development strategy for a small-sized health care company. At that time, my focus was on human resource development, and the main methodology at the research laboratory at which I worked was job analysis and competency modeling (McClelland & Boyatzis, 1982; McClelland, 1973). Our research team of three researchers and one research assistant was helping a small enterprise that was about to introduce a chatbot technology to their customer service department. Our team was required to develop a competency model, as the company was about to adopt text mining technology (one of the big data technologies) and automate a small part of customer services' work by building a database based on past customers' questions. The service that the company provided was mostly concerned with weight-watching programs. The diet consultants working in the company answered the questions from their customers about meals—for example, what kind of meal would be allowed at midnight. The problem was that the customers were allowed to ask the questions anytime, anywhere, which caused the consultants a lot of stress, and ultimately contributed to the increasing turnover rate.

The executives in the company grew anxious about this problem and decided to adopt a chatbot technology to run an automated customer service program. Their intent was clear, concise, and rational. The high employee turnover brought myriad side effects, including lowering the overall performance of the organization and threatening the sustainability of the organization (Hom et al., 2017). As their business was in the middle of a rapid growth phase, their anxiety was perfectly understandable. Also, interviewing the executives in order to refine their old company vision led me to understand their strong attachment to their company and passion to better their business; their business was their life. Interestingly, all the executives were female, and none of them exhibited any problem with their work-life balance. They were that committed to their work.

Because of the scope of the project, the research team worked closely with program developers, participating in several meetings. We discussed the plans for introducing the program in the workplace. Our work was more aligned with dividing the responsibilities between the automated workforce (in this case, the chatbot program) and the human workforce (the diet consultants). We interviewed every employee at the company in order to break down their roles and responsibilities into several sets of competencies and to come up with newer competency models. As the executives wanted us to develop a future plan for automating the workforce, we suggested some ideas as well. The project was successful. We developed our plans and models within the designated time frame, and the executives were satisfied with our results. The company launched the chatbot program immediately after the end of the project and used the competency model we developed for staff recruitment and evaluation.

Even though the program was a success, the experience haunted me. For the first time in my life, I felt shocked, observing how easy and fast it is to automate the workforce. In particular, I was astounded when the program developers shared a remarkably short timeframe with the executives. I assumed that plenty of time would be invested in developing the chatbot. However, my assumption was shattered as the developers came up with the prototype of the program within a month and assured the client that they would be able to develop this technology within three to four months.

I could not get over the feeling that I derived from this experience; mixed with guilt, the unease I felt lasted a long time. My interior monologue was filled with innumerable inquiries. The experience completely shook my belief about instrumentalized learning, as I sympathized with the "visceral feeling" (Bateson, 1991, p. 171) of people in response to the techno-centric workplace transformation. Learning had nothing to do with their development; learning was just used as a way to assure that what they feared was not going to happen, and I felt perturbed, as the original intention to develop the human development strategy that may help employees figure out their positions in the face of machinic workforce or matchless competitors in terms of productivity did not seem to be a "humanizing" effort to me. From my perspective, what the strategy was doing, in part, was planting the worry of getting replaced by the machinic workforce if the human workforce could not keep up with the changes.

What disturbed me was the pace of the change initiatives. If it does not take that much time and effort to develop a program that inevitably replaces most of the menial laborers, how can the employees process the abrupt changes? If the employees are laid off in such a quick way because of the managerial decision to reduce the labor cost, can they survive the transition? If so, what kind of learning should they do? Would they even have the energy to learn something new to survive in such a context? In the "job-less" capitalist society (Peters, 2020), would people keep learning to upskill or develop themselves? Would learning mean anything in a society where the meaning of labor, or the "blessing of the labor" (Berkowitz, 2018, p. 345), is eradicated?

Undergoing: What Do I Desire to See in the Future?

The perturbation that I felt from the experience led me to recognize my specific desire for the future of work—a future of work with vitality. In a sense, the disquiet I felt, as well as my questions on the meaning of learning, led me to crystallize the way in which I formulated my relationship with the future. In questioning the role of adult learning in the future of work context, I encountered the unknown embedded in the process, and I barely recognized my deeply programmed desire—to be meaningful, different, energetic. That is why I was so disturbed by the image of the stalled future that I experienced as a result of my research.

According to Deleuze and Guattari (1972/1983), *desire* does not necessarily mean "lack" but "motivation"; it is a driving force that lets individuals seek a meaningful connection with their system or surrounding environment. In this regard, my desire, or the driving force to construct the vital future of work, surely is constituted by my reflective thoughts, implying some pertinence to my environment or system. The environment, however, is hard to discern, as it works like a "smoke ring" (Bateson, 1991, p. 223), which is hardly recognizable because of its airy nature that makes it blend with the surrounding elements. However, through the endless, continuous, introspective effort, the distinction of the environment is possible, just as the smoke ring has its "duration, location and a certain degree of separation by virtue of its inturned motion" (p. 223). According to Bateson, the efforts come in a brief flash of awareness, when the individual maps the encounters of difference onto one's mind and creates another layer of worldview. This poetic description of the smoke ring connects with what Dewey said about reflection: that the hardly conspicuous yet still existing nature of environment requires a conscious effort to recognize, think, or contemplate, through which, in Deweyan language, reflective thought emerges (d'Agnes, 2016).

In an attempt to sketch my environment and how it connects with my desire, I will, later on in this chapter, elaborate on what I inherited from my cultural and personal background, and how those inheritances affected my current relationship with learning. In the process of unfolding my inquiry around the future of work, I came to defamiliarize my deeply ingrained assumptions, beliefs, and understanding around the future—future for vitality—and began to wonder about my future-self. As a doctoral student who studies and learns about learning, theory of mind, and change, this moment of crisis may be inevitable. In the process of defamiliarization, I stumbled upon moments of loss because I felt that the difference that I noticed made my past self—as a good, studious student—look strange.

I was born and raised in South Korea and lived there until 2019. It is inevitable that my cultural background is deeply ingrained in my inquiry, which seeks to shed light on the role of learning. Recalling, imagining, and defamiliarizing learning surfaces my parents' history and their relationship with learning. My perception of the South Korean context and my parents' lived experience is coded into my being and knowing. The ongoing process of my research constantly brings up such codes, which are thrown into the questions whenever I encounter new thinking. My moments of crisis may be understood as encountering "news of boundaries—news of the contexts of difference" (Bateson, 1991, p. 219). It may be referred to as triple-loop learning (Torbert, 2004) or Bateson's (1991) Learning Level III. However it is defined, this process of inquiry is still ongoing, and in forming the relationship with the future ahead of me, my system, and the global milieu, I encounter moments of enlightenment, for which I believe generative knowing plays a role.

Before moving into my vignettes, one thing that I would like to highlight is that the later sections of this chapter, which bring a special focus to my experiences with learning that are inherited and culturally embedded, are not all of my South Korean culture. South Korean culture is much more complex, but for the purposes of this inquiry, a slice of my perception toward the complexity is represented and reframed through the lens of generative knowing. As I *In-scend* beneath my cultural history, I may find more pain than joy, and that finding is enlightening and frees me in ways that I will reveal later. The purpose of this chapter is not to devalue the hyper-competitive educational environment of South Korea, nor is it meant to criticize the obsession with education prevalent in South Korea. As Braidotti (2019) said, it is necessary to respect the complex singularity, and, given its tumultuous history and geographical location, South Korea's education fever needs to be justified, not condemned. I highlight the ultra-competitiveness of Korean society in order to provide context to how my past conceptualization of learning was, how my desire is formulated in the past, and how it affects my being and knowing. My intention is clear: Surfacing my experience and cultural background is "to look the past and the future to situate analyses" (Tuck & Yang, 2014, p. 231) and not to describe my community as damaged or broken.

What will be discussed in the following section is very personal. I hesitated a great deal about disclosing my experience and personal background; I was reluctant to show my vulnerabilities. I was afraid that some may argue that this way of narrating myself would be self-proclaiming. Ultimately, however, I viewed these voices of doubt as a repressive power that I internalized and felt that presenting my story would somehow be an emancipatory process of my own making, constituting my becoming-nomad. As such, these vignettes illuminate the process of my becoming a researcher of learning, in the post-human predicament.

My Heritage: Learning to Survive, Desire to Survive

My parents were education enthusiasts who worked most of their lives in order to pay tuition and support their family. They believed that education was the sole route to climb up the ladder. Both were first-generation college graduates. Both majored in electronic engineering, and were engineers employed by big corporations at that time. Another commonality between them was their unfortunate and involuntary job loss. My dad was employed by the South Korean branch of a global software enterprise in 1984 until he lost his job because of the 1997 Korean financial crisis (see Figure 7.1).

My mom was one of the first-generation female engineers hired by one of the largest corporations of that time, or arguably, one of the major economic drivers in South Korea around the 1980s (see Figure 7.2). She lost her job one day before her marriage in 1987.

My parents' work experience influenced their attitudes toward learning, which inevitably became my heritage. My dad, as a front-end engineer, managed the corporation's products—mainly electronic cash registers—in theme parks. Until he left his job in 1997 to start his own business, around the onset

Figure 7.1. A Collage of Photos of My Dad Working in the Company

Note: (clockwise from top right) Group photo taken during his business trip to the headquarters of his company in the United States; the other two photos are of him working in the corporation with his colleagues.

of the Asian financial crisis, he kept studying and learning new software, technologies, and English, in order to keep up with the development of personal computers and communication tools, and to become business-savvy. Back then, personal computers were beginning to be common in households, and he tried his best to learn the new technology. Nonetheless, it was not always easy to do double-duty. He was also the oldest child in a low-income family and had six sisters and brothers who needed his help. Regardless, he continued his effort to adapt to the changing environment, but his effort became useless thanks to the national bankruptcy. Back then the company, according to my dad, was not so strategically adaptive to the changing circumstances. In fact, the global enterprise struggled to adapt to computerized products

Figure 7.2. A Collage of Photos Showing My Mom Working in the Corporation

Note: The two upper photos show her in the early 20s, and the bottom photo shows her enjoying a corporate retreat. We can see in these photos that all of her colleagues were male.

in the 1970s, although it eventually shifted gears to electronic machines (Rosenbloom, 2000).

My mom, who was the first woman engineer among 200 newcomers to the company in 1981, strived to secure her job in her male-dominated workplace for seven years. Her effort came to nothing when she got fired one day before her marriage, in 1987. She remembers being asked by her boss when she first went to the office, "Did you graduate summa cum laude?" At that time, women being hired not as secretaries but as engineers—or, in her own words, "the real job"—were unique. In fact, in 1980, only 3.7% of women were hired to fill professional technical positions (Park, 1990). Although she was hired as an engineer, my mom's main job at first was procuring materials for constructing subways or making robotic software. The fact that she was spotted by the then-director when he was forming a team proves her high level of competence. Nevertheless, she lost her job in 1987 literally because she got married. Although she appealed to the human resources manager, stating that she wanted to continue her career regardless of her marital status, she found a blank letter of resignation on her desk one day before her wedding reception. She told me that she could not even retrieve her belongings or hand over her work to her successor.

My dad worked to stay literate in a techno-centric business, and my mom struggled to find and hold her position in a male-dominated workspace. Sadly, no matter how hard they tried, both were defeated by the system. Their future was not always rosy. Despite the encounter, however, they endured the *Ruptures* of massive, economic crisis and gender discrimination, as they refused to sink into despair. Their smoke rings were full of responsibilities. They started their own business and continued to survive. Their new projects were their two daughters and, just as they had before, they diligently took care of their projects. Their priority has been their daughters since then. One of them was taught the violin, as she showed some talent in music, even at a young age. It was good news to them, because gender did not seem to matter much in the arts. The other daughter (me) was always a problem for them. According to them, I did not show any interest in music or other fields, so they just let me study and get prepared for an unknown future. Their decision was a pretty normal in South Korea, especially among the parents with the tertiary education experience: the more educated parents are, the stronger their educational aspirations are manifested in parenting (Kim & Bang, 2017). In fact, my parents struggled to let my career aspirations emerge by trying out diverse educational opportunities, which was normalized by then-parental culture, and apparently neither art nor music evoked my interest. Consequently, I just followed what others did, without any specific deliberation of what I wanted to become.

The issue of how to efficiently prepare for the future has been the main impetus for opportunity and growth for South Korea. After the end of Japanese colonization in 1945 and the Korean War that followed in 1950, South Korean society experienced miraculously rapid economic development, and education fueled this growth. From the country with a literacy rate of 22% in

1945, South Korea now has the highest rate of tertiary education completion among the OECD countries, as 65% of young adults have completed higher education (Jones, 2013). The rapid growth of South Korean society, which is called the "Miracle on the Han River," gave birth to the notion of "every child can prosper," and this was coupled with the massive introduction of Western egalitarianism in society (Park, 1990). The 1997 Asian Financial Crisis also caused the education fever to intensify. The heightened insecurity of life had caused individuals to focus more on education. To secure a well-paid job was and still is viewed as of utmost importance, and education is believed to guarantee the path to security. Fueled by this belief, Korean children have been sent to numerous *hagwons* (private cram schools) in order to get into the prestigious and elite universities—"SKY" universities (Seoul National University, Korea University, and Yonsei University)—which were believed to be an absolute necessity for a social climber (Anderson & Kohler, 2013).

South Korean parents' high education fever epitomizes how socially constructed desire is. Education has been touted as a way to upgrade the socioeconomic status at the backdrop of Confucian culture, which adores learning (Lee, 2017). My parents were born and raised in the era of rapid industrialization and military administration. They were taught and disciplined to learn to succeed, prosper, and survive. That they were able to secure jobs in big business proved that their investment was spot on, which inevitably shaped their beliefs toward learning. Such a belief system, which constitutes a major part of my heritage, was developed at the intersections of their personal upbringings, culture, and education background, and, in a sense, formed a cycle of desire investment. Education has been a vehicle for materializing their individual desire of enduring and even positively contributing to the system. In other words, their life choices show "that . . . desire is positively invested in the system" (Smith, 2011, p. 74).

Undeniably, my parents were among them. Despite their strong belief in a future of vitality—a future full of potential—they were not free from the grid of desire. As a result, my upbringing did not allow me to form an affirmative relationship with learning; my relationship with learning was mostly enforced and inescapable, yet pivotal and significant. Luckily, I got my bachelor's and master's degrees from one of the SKY universities. My parents worked at least 12 hours a day, running small retail shops and commuting for 2 hours, in order to give me the best educational experience; ostensibly, in some sense, their work paid off. When I was a child, during my parent's business hours, I was sent to different *hagwons* in addition to going to a school. According to my mom's memory, she sent me to the English *hagwon* as a way to outsource the care service it provided and enhance my English skills, because at that time English was deemed a symbol of socio-economic status (Chung & Choi, 2016). Because English was believed to be an essential tool to succeed in the globalization era, the *hagwon* was always populated, even with its absurd pedagogy. I remember being severely punished when I could not get all the answers right in my vocabulary test in my English *hagwon*. The stress was intense. I was even diagnosed with stress-induced gastritis when I was 10 years old. Notably and unfortunately, this narrative of struggle is not uncommon in South Korea; I believe every South Korean has their version of this story in South Korea's ultra-competitive environment, which normalizes a winner-takes-all mindset.

The whole experience led me to major in English education for my bachelor's degree, as English was, ironically, one of my strengths because of the harsh training. Although the university provided me with good-quality faculty and classes that allowed me to gain different insights regarding education, for me, learning was still a skill-acquisition tool rather than a route to human maturation or development. I believe that my learning experience during my university years, despite that period being very valuable in nourishing my knowledge base, was not penetrating enough to change any deeply programmed relationships with learning; that was influenced by my parents' teaching and guidance.

My Present: Reorienting My Desire from Survival to Generativity

Sketching my smoke ring through the vignettes of my parents and myself indicates that it is not so uncommon for one to be immersed in preparation for the future, with the affirmative belief in a future with potential. Ironically, these attunements to the future often diminish the richness of the present. The astute decision to make the future fruitful sacrifices the living present. Dewey (1938) also pointed out that appropriating the present only to get ready for the future is itself paradoxical. This way of preparation only "omits and even shuts out the very conditions by which a person can be prepared for his future" (Dewey, 1938, p. 49). Preparing for the future at the expense of the present narrows the full meaning each present experience grants us; in order for individuals to be fully immersed in the texture of the present, "attentive care must be devoted to the conditions which give each present experience a worthwhile meaning" (Dewey, 1938, p. 49).

To view learning as only for the future, built upon the desire to be ready, or to become prepared for the unknown precarity, is to reduce the complexity embedded within the future potential and to exclude the possibility for individuals to undergo the present. Undergoing, as aforementioned, assumes the transformation of ingrained assumptions or beliefs. It requires the individual to be receptive, adequately yielding one's self through controlled activity (Dewey, 1938, p. 55). The visceral feeling that I experienced let me confront my habitual thinking around the role of learning—as an instrument to survive the harsh, competitive environment of the South Korean education system. My experience as a research assistant on one project reveals how instrumentalized learning had been accepted without question, in hopes of getting the workforce prepared for the unknown future. This, in fact, is a tip of normalized conception in South Korean culture in which education has been conceptualized and utilized as one easy route to upgrading one's socio-economic status. In this regard, learning in South Korea is directed toward the future of oneself without the full appreciation of the given present.

Entering the scene of questioning, thinking, and undergoing the future of work, in the process of undergoing work for a future, I found the bits and pieces that are embedded in myself and my smoke rings. My parents hold some pieces of the bits that form my beliefs regarding the future. Their constant eagerness to re-invest themselves in the system was transmitted to me, as a belief that learning new skills and language is necessary and indispensable in order to survive a harsh, competitive environment. Their relentless endeavors to provide for their daughters the best they could taught those daughters to believe in themselves, which is shown in their life-long commitment to the creative fields. In my case, my past desire to learn was constructed and conditioned in line with the ultra-competitiveness of the South Korean context; I invested in my desire to learn through instrumentalized learning. I was desperate to keep up with future demands, and my desire was associated with my parents' desire as well as society's vision of the future: no learning, no survival. My academic success and studious persona show how I was a voluntary, fervent follower of such a desired framework.

Experiencing a slice of the future of work, dipping my toe in working with algorithms, I became aware of my desire to learn and the embedded system that I breathed in. The system that I was supposed to feel comfortable in now felt strange, and the perturbation that I felt throughout the experience, treating learning as I used to, led me to recognize the fact that I no longer want to endure the systematically programmed desire to learn for the sake of someone else's view of the future. In some sense, undergoing the experience has reoriented my desire to learn differently, toward the vitality that focuses more on the whole-person development and ontological sense of learning.

Undergoing the Future of Work: The Scene for Generative Knowing

According to various adult learning theories, social prescriptions are what adults need to reflect on, endure, or even resist, as the due process means learning (i.e., Bateson, 1991; Kegan, 1982; Torbert, 2004). During the process, one might feel the loss of identity and operating ground, as learning requires a departure from the comfort zone. As such, learning is not for everyone (Nicolaides, 2015). In this context, adult learning means reorienting one's desire, as desire is "a transversal ontological force that displaces categorical distinctions" (Braidotti, 2019, p. 47). This is because desire is socially constructed, and reorienting desire means mobilizing the force so that individuals can move toward positivity and self-expression. Generative knowing touches upon the process of reorienting desires toward affirmative and generative pathways. Generative knowing explicitly restores the emancipatory intention of adult learning in a way in which learning contributes to the flourishing of oneself as well as the system by acknowledging the process of one's becoming, embodiedness, and embeddedness.

The force of technological development, with its nature of irreversibility, ubiquity, and instantaneity, epitomizes the unknown of the present. According to Braidotti (2019), the advent of anthropomorphic images of algorithms (i.e., Siri or Alexa) situates humanity in the "posthuman predicament" (p. 8). That is, human-ness, which is supposed to belong exclusively to humanity, now manifests in technology as well. This unprecedented condition creates the foreign subject-matter—that is, technology that used to exist inert and without agency all of a sudden becomes an important agent. This new condition, in turn, calls the meaning of human-ness into question. What does it mean to become human, if technology can imitate what we think, perceive, and understand? The image of workplaces where individual lawyers get help from algorithms to review documents (Remus & Levy, 2016), or Uber drivers are constantly nudged to drive more than they want (Rosenblat, 2018), shake the assumption that the human is the ultimate decision-maker in the socio-technical interface. Although the future that has been depicted in Hollywood sci-fi movies, where malicious cybernetic machines attack humans, is less likely to happen, mathematical evaluation models, or algorithms, that are used in everyday work settings—checking grammar, transcribing meeting notes, or even matching preferred work positions—are highly likely to intrude in our daily lives.

In this context, the future of work signifies a reconfiguration of human conditions. In a larger milieu of change, including the introduction and expansion of artificial intelligence (AI), algorithms, or other smart technologies in our daily lives, the foundational beliefs and assumptions around human conditions become unfamiliar. In this new setting, new thinking is necessary as a path to depart from human-centeredness. Nonetheless, sketching new territories in which human actors and non-human actors are equally privileged poses an ethical question: Who is responsible for the flaws in making decisions? For instance, algorithms that were used in the hiring process of technology giant Amazon insidiously perpetuated racial bias (Tambe et al., 2019). In this case, who is accountable for such flaws? Is it the engineer's mistake? Is this an issue of the absence of governance?

To complicate the matter, what people fail to recognize is what technology cannot do. Broussard (2018) brazenly criticizes such a tendency, calling it techno-chauvinism. People have iteratively chosen convenience at the expense of their integrity, making the false assumption that technology will free us all, only to uncover that techno-chauvinistic thinking sustains inequality that has long existed in the society. Nonetheless, because of their purported objectivity, algorithmic recommendations are often received as those from "credentialized experts, the scientific method, common sense or the word of God" (Gillespie, 2014, p. 168). With the new presence and the power of algorithms, the habitual way of living in the human condition is not so familiar anymore, and deserves exploration. That is, ontological questions arise as a response to the departure from the anthropocentric worldview; people begin to question their subjectivities, asking themselves, "Am I a robot?" (Braidotti, 2019, p. viii).

According to Danaher (2019), this will be the beacon of another era, particularly in terms of working society. That is, "Machines are being created to anticipate our wants and needs and provide us with all the entertainment, food, and distraction we could ever desire . . . . We are moving from the Anthropocene to what might be called the *robocene*" (p. 2, italics in original). Some may point out that this way of interpreting today's change might be exaggerated, as historically there have been technologically induced workplace changes, but with less disruptiveness, as opposed to what they claim to be. The invention of individualized computers and the massive introduction of word processors promised a "paperless office" in the late 1980s (Haigh, 2006). The introduction of the internet claimed to bring a "New Economy," wherein knowledge becomes the social capital (Thurow, 1999) and the visionary image of "a new world beyond government" (Broussard, 2018, p. 5).

Even so, the massive shift in the socio-technical interface, thanks to the potential expansion of computational workforces, seemingly excites the public. On the online video platform YouTube, entering the search term "future of work," there appear a substantial number of documentaries with titles such as *The Big Debate about the Future of Work, Explained*; *The Future of Work: Is Your Job Safe?*; *The Future of Work: Will Our Children Be Prepared?*; *What Will the Future of Jobs Be Like?* Diverse speculations on the future of work are suggested in order to better understand and prepare for the uncertainty. In a similar vein, there is a plethora of white papers on the future of work, and how learning new skills and tuning to lifelong learning would help individuals keep up with the technologically induced shift (Deloitte Global, 2018; International Labor Organization, 2019; McKinsey Global Institute, 2018; Organization for Economic Cooperation and Development, 2019; World Economic Forum, 2016).

The torrent of exploratory questions around the future of work shows how this brewing change may become "every opportunity that occurs within their practical activities for developing curiosity and susceptibility to intellectual problems" (Dewey, 1910/2007, p. 70). This intellectual problem deserves an agent that operates within the new conceptual territory or a "conceptual persona (Deleuze & Guattari, 1994, p.62)." This is the place where the posthuman comes in as a figuration that enables multiple imaginings regarding the future of work. Borrowing Deleuze's language, Braidotti (2019) suggests posthuman as a conceptual persona in such a posthuman predicament. Deleuze and Guattari (1994) understand philosophy as a plane of immanence, where different concepts are laid out and new concepts are constantly created and invented. On this plane, the conceptual persona is a figurative subject who engages in the process of laying out and creating concepts, or, simply put, thinking. According to Deleuze, Plato transmitted his philosophy through the image of Socrates, Nietzsche made Dionysus, and Descartes created the Cartesian man. In order to address the complexity of power, Braidotti suggests posthuman as a conceptual persona of the current settings. By setting such a conceptual persona, people can "enter a thought that 'slides' with new substances of being" (Deleuze & Guattari, 1994, p. 71) and surf across the waves of thoughts more freely.

Deleuze's metaphor of the thinker as a surfer may strengthen the understanding of how the posthuman image works as a conceptual persona in the future of work context. That is, posthumans "expose the repressive structures of dominant subject formations (*poestas*) but also the affirmative and transformative visions of the subject as both grounded, flowing or in process (*potentia*)" (Braidotti, 2019, p. 136). Bringing the posthuman as a conceptual persona into the future of work context may expose the flow of a transforming subject (how they are in the process of changing), and not restrict the subject as the end or the beginning of the transformative process. Multiple potentialities embedded in the future of work discourse would thereby thrive.

Generative knowing, as a nomadic theory of adult learning, resists the normative understanding and practices of adult learning—mainly, commodification and instrumentalization of learning. In order to explain how generative knowing theory fits into the context of the future of work, it is important to figure out how learning is treated in that context. The bits and pieces of narratives on how technology catalyze the changes in the workplace generate bifurcated reactions to upcoming changes—either techno-phobic or techno-philiac (Bogue, 2019). The either/or reactions to such techno-centric transformations overlook the affirmative flow of power that may be generated throughout the techno-centric transformation by paying more attention to what technology would do to humans, or vice versa, situating both subjects (humans and machines) in a winner-takes-all dynamic on the basis of monopolizing the repressive aspects of power. Such dynamics presuppose an instrumentalizing view, which often disregards the possibility of cooperation between two subjects and hinders the imagination of the third way out of the unknown. In the techno-phobic future of work, individuals are coded and scored, beyond their cognition, trapping them in an algorithmic society (i.e., Broussard, 2018; Rosenblat, 2018; Stiegler, 2019); in the techno-philiac future of work, technology frees individuals from unnecessary tasks and enhances their well-being through the gain of valuable time (i.e., Danaher, 2019).

The commonality of the two different strands of the either-or view, whether it suggests a positive or pessimistic perspective, is that both presuppose the movement of power that "implies processes of normalization, modification, modeling and information that bear on language, perception, desire, movement, etc." (Deleuze & Guattari, 1987, p. 458). That is, in both views, humans and technology are said to mutually affect, and are affected, in a way that aligns with their desires: technology-free-human or humans-obey-technology.

In this context, the way in which learning is treated and imagined in current literature regarding the future of work does not escape from the desire framework. In both scenarios, be it technology-free-human or humans-obey-technology, the underlying desire is to control and manage the uncertainty residing in the ever-intimate relationship between technology and human. Learning, in this regard, is appropriated as a resourceful way to better decode the uncertainty. That is, learning is conceptualized as a supporter of the desire cycle embedded in the future of work, by bearing the functional, competent individuals who can understand and serve the system well; naturally, the external pull for preparation and readiness are privileged in conceptualizing learning in the future of work context. The focus is less on the internal motivation of individual development and maturity and more on the externally imposed wants and needs. This is what generative knowing resists: the insidious desiring mechanism that the discourse imposes upon individuals, and producing them as a desiring machine. Deleuze and Guattari (1987) warned of such an insidious "perpetuation or conservation" of state, or institutional power, by shedding light on how the state affects individuals' "voluntary servitude" (p. 359). Individuals are programmed and conditioned to have desires, and to think that such desires are their voluntary choices, no matter how the society imposes those desires upon them.

Notably, preparing for the unknown future, to be on a par with fast-paced technological development, has been imperative for individuals striving to survive the complexity of the future of work. At the same time, technology is deemed as what humans should utilize, instrumentalize, or colonize, in order not to be surveilled. This way of situating humans in the governing position and imposing the need to master and govern the feedback loop of decision-making in the socio-technical landscape has actually been common in our history. According to Taylor (2020), in Heidegger's depiction of cybernetic representation, "human beings create technologies, which, in turn, recreate human beings" (p. 6). That is, human beings become "prostheses of the machines they create" (p. 7) through their effort to master and control the feedback loop. It is interesting to note how Deleuze and Guattari (1987) made a similar point regarding the relationship that individuals form with machines, that in the industrial culture, human beings become workers or users of the machine, and "he or she is subjected *to* the machine and no longer enslaved *by* the machine" (p. 457; emphasis in original). That is, humans are required to master the machines rather than live with them or become them.

The habitual thinking that emerges out of the desire to master and command deters the possible affirmative future that technology may open up. That is, the computational, logical algorithms that assist reasoning or thinking would "open new channels for messages that sustain life" (Taylor, 2020, p. 10). Algorithms, if treated well and ethically, would present a better future. With new thinking, we may be able to live with algorithms or enjoy mutual attunement. However, on the threshold of old, habitual thoughts and new, emerging thinking, people prefer habitual thinking as it economizes the operations of the mind (Bateson, 1991). The fear manifested in the future of work literature is what people are accustomed to showing, in the face of the unknown. The economization of mind, averting the uncertainty, may be explained by people's developmental capacity (Nicolaides, 2015). Although the habitual thinking does not fully address the singularity of the future of work context that we should deal with, it still attracts a profusion of economized minds that choose to stay in the realm of their comfort zone. The economization of minds can be translated into Deweyan language as a halting of intellectual energy; that is, such choices break the balance of curiosity and susceptibility, and would rather give up the circulation of intellectual energy, obstructing reflection. Some would argue that the future of work literature privileges new skills, new digital literacy, and new work management skills as necessary to cope with the new conditions (i.e., Newport, 2016; Wergin,

2019), and thus positioning such views as habitual thinking would constitute unfair denigration. Yet this way of privileging skill acquisition fortifies the culture that instrumentalizes learning and sacrifices the present with the belief in the "better" future, only to limit its potential. This is in stark contrast to what Dewey (1938) talked about regarding undergoing experience. In undergoing experience, individuals uncover new ways of thinking that go beyond the habitual either/or view. In this regard, what Braidotti (2019) insisted—becoming posthuman trying a conceptual persona that travels freely to acknowledge the repressive and potential aspects of power—would help us avoid the economization of minds.

What Dewey argued about—"caring attentively to the present condition"—aligns with what generative knowing attunes to: let individuals immerse themselves in the play of the all-ready and not-yet potential of the present condition, the constant intra-activity between the not-yet-actualized and the actualized, the virtual and the actual (Braidotti, 2019; Deleuze & Guattari, 1987). The future of work encompasses potential changes that are presented, through images in different types of media and by new metaphorical languages, to indicate the new epoch—Schwab's fourth industrial revolution (2016), Brynjolfsson and McAfee's machinic age (2014), Danaher's robocene (2019), or even Briadotti's posthuman predicament (2019). The changes that evoke such new languages are materialized in reality. Thus, the future of work context is a mixture of the not-yet actualized (virtual) and the already actualized (actual). As such, the context is an amalgam of the familiar and the strange. In order for individuals to undergo the future of work, not to sacrifice their present for the better future but to face and feel the unknown and to resist institutionalized power, generative knowing is a way to make new things. That is why I argue that the future of work is a great playing field for generative knowing to expand and circulate intellectual energy as ways of being and becoming.

Conclusion

Admittedly, the whole process of writing this piece cuts through my meaning-making by *In-scending* into my parent's history, their life-decisions, and their visions, which left a large yet shadowy mark on my ways of knowing, doing, and being. Reframing my parents' history, asking them questions about their intentions and the desire behind their parenting as the youngest child of our family, deepening the mutual understanding of our past came as a unique yet vitalizing experience. On the one hand, I am their youngest child, meaning that my biological inheritance associated with their "descriptive prescriptions, injunctions" forms the basis of my epistemology (Bateson, 1991, p. 178). On the other hand, my unique and different interaction with the environment adds a different dimension to my epistemology, generating a different sense of self than what my parents would expect me to become. My choice of being committed to learning beyond education and the hard sciences is in opposition to my parents' desire; the choice emerges from a willing, intentional engagement with the stuff of my lived experience, past, present, and future.

I believe that my desire to learn is more fluid than fixed; my relationship with learning in the process of inquiring about the future of work puts what I am becoming at the center. I am inquiring beneath the experience of intersections of ceasing to be what I was and becoming what I will be. My not-yet-actualized (or virtual) self is the complex singularity, which can be understood as an arrangement of one's past and present (Deleuze & Guattari, 1987). My virtual self is still constituted by both my past-self as a good, studious child in South Korea who meticulously searched only for the known facts and followed the right answers, and my current self as an inquirer who wants to look through to the unknown.

With the blessing of advanced communication technology, our family often enjoys hour-long conversations on Zoom, and we always conclude our talks with our gratitude for the present in which we find ourselves. I often find this moment amazing, as I am well aware of my parents' financial distress and the trajectory of their overcoming those struggles by themselves; they are still running small retail shops in South Korea, even during the COVID-19 pandemic era, and are still figuring their way out of the unexpected impasses imposed on them. I dare to say that what my parents taught me, in this regard, is their affirmative ethics toward the unknown future; they have been resilient throughout the course of their lives, showing the utmost support and unconditional care for both of their daughters—daughters who are still struggling to find their own paths in the fields of art and education. In this sense, my desire is still being constructed by the system that I was born and raised into, and the other systems where I am learning to become free. This means that my self-conception and my relationship to learning, which undergirds my inquiry toward the future of work, is not a static point. It is an immanent (re)arrangement of my desire. Of course, elucidating this immanent arrangement requires a deep reflection, a free circulation of my intellectual energy without any temporal or systemic boundaries.

This chapter can be better understood as an example of how I remember, imagine, and defamiliarize the complexity of my singularity, and how the process contributes to shaping my imagination toward a generative future of work. As mentioned earlier, different factors contribute to the (re)configuration of the complexity of my singularity, as time sequences are multi-dimensional. My past and present, my actual (ceasing-to-be) and virtual (not-yet-to-be), are important elements for me to surf across and play within the future of work context. The question still remains: Who am I becoming as a researcher, activist, and meaningful participant in a world unfolding in a way that cannot be fore-known? In the future of work context into which I am attempting to plug generative knowing, a new socio-technical complexity is emerging with the ever-deepening relationship between human and machine. The context deserves a new theoretical engagement, as the rapidity of technological development allows individuals to lose the capacity to think through theoretically and places the segment of humanity in danger of living in the era of "systemic stupidity" (Stiegler, 2019, p. 34). In aligning myself with the affirmative ethics put forth by Braidotti (2019) and re-orienting my desire toward not-fore-known potential, I work with generative learning as a trustworthy accompaniment as it lets me muddle through the complexity.

Note:

1. Special thanks to my Summer 2021 writing group (Wendy Anderson, Laronda Brown, Heather Lindell, and Shannon Perry), as well as Sunny Lee in South Korea, for their thoughtful reviews and comments.

References

Anderson, T., & Kohler, H. P. (2013). Education fever and the East Asian fertility puzzle: A case study of low fertility in South Korea. *Asian Population Studies, 9*(2), 196–215.
Bateson, G. (1991). *A sacred unity: Further steps to an ecology of mind.* Harper.
Berkowitz, R. (2018). The Singularity and the Human Condition. *Philosophy Today, 62*(2). https://doi.org/10.5840/philtoday2018522214

Bogue, R. (2019). *Thinking with Deleuze*. Edinburgh University Press.

Braidotti, R. (2019). *Posthuman knowledge*. Polity Press.

Bridle, J. (2018). *New dark age: Technology and the end of the future*. Verso Books.

Broussard, M. (2018). *Artificial unintelligence: How computers misunderstand the world*. MIT Press.

Brynjolfsson, E., & McAfee, A. (2014). *The second machine age: Work, progress, and prosperity in a time of brilliant technologies*. WW Norton & Company.

Chung, J., & Choi, T. (2016). English education policies in South Korea: Planned and enacted. In *English language education policy in asia* (pp. 281–299). Berlin: Springer International.

Crawford, K. (2021). *The atlas of AI*. Yale University Press.

d'Agnese, V. (2016). Undergoing, mystery, and half-knowledge: John Dewey's disquieting side. *Studies in philosophy and education, 35*(2), 195–214. https://doi.org/10.1007/s11217-015-9483-2

Danaher, J. (2019). *Automation and Utopia: Human flourishing in a world without work*. Harvard University Press.

Deleuze, G. & Guattari, F. (1983). *Anti-oedipus: Capitalism and schizophrenia*. University of Minnesota Press. (R. Hurley, M. Seem & H. R. Lane Trans.). (Original work published in 1972).

Deleuze, G., & Guattari, F. (1987). *A thousand plateaus: Capitalism and schizophrenia* (B. Massumi, Trans.). University of Minnesota Press. (Original work published 1980)

Deleuze, G., & Guattari, F. (1994). *What is philosophy?* (H. Tomlinson, & G. Burchell, Trans.). Columbia University Press. (Original work published 1991)

Deloitte Global, & The Global Business Coalition for Education. (2018). *Preparing tomorrow's workforce for the fourth industrial revolution* [Executive summary]. https://www2.deloitte.com/global/en/pages/about-deloitte/articles/gx-preparing-tomorrow-workforce-for-the-fourth-industrial-revolution.html

Dewey, J. (1934). *Art as experience*. Macmillan.

Dewey, J. (1938). *Experience and Education*. Touchstone.

Dewey, J. (2007). *How we think*. Digireads.com Publishing. (Original work published 1910)

Gillespie, T. (2014). The relevance of algorithms. In T. Gillespie, P. J. Boczkowski, & K. A. Foot (Eds.), *Media technologies: Essays on communication, materiality, and society*. MIT Press.

Haigh, T. (2006). Remembering the office of the future: The origins of word processing and office automation. *IEEE Annals of the History of Computing, 28*(4), 6–31. http://doi.org/10.1109/MAHC.2006.70

Hom, P. W., Lee, T. W., Shaw, J. D., & Hausknecht, J. P. (2017). One hundred years of employee turnover theory and research. *Journal of Applied Psychology, 102*(3), 530. https://doi.org/10.1037/apl0000103

International Labor Organization (2019). *Work for a brighter future: Global commission on the future of work* [Executive summary].

Jones, R. S. (2013). Education reform in Korea. *OECD Economics Department Working Papers, No. 1067*. OECD Publishing. http://dx.doi.org/10.1787/5k43nxs1t9vh-en

Kegan, R. (1982). *The evolving self: Problem and process in human development*. Harvard University Press.

Kim, J-S., & Bang, H. (2017). Education fever: Korean parents' aspirations for their children's schooling and future career. *Pedagogy, Culture & Society, 25*(2), 207–224. http://doi.org.10.1080/14681366.2016.1252419

Kolb, D. A. (1984). *Experiential learning: Experience as the source of learning and development*. Prentice-Hall.

Lee, J. K. (2017). *Education fever and happiness in Korean higher education* (ED574875). ERIC. https://files.eric.ed.gov/fulltext/ED574875.pdf

McClelland, D. C. (1973). Testing for competence rather than for "intelligence." *American Psychologist, 28*(1), 1–14. https://doi.org/10.1037/h0034092

McClelland, D. C., & Boyatzis, R. E. (1982). Leadership motive pattern and long-term success in management. *Journal of Applied psychology, 67*(6), 737. https://doi.org/10.1037/0021-9010.67.6.737

McKinsey Global Institute (2018). *Skill shift: Automation and the future of the workforce*. Retrieved November 23, 2019, from https://www.mckinsey.com/featured-insights/future-of-work/skill-shift-automation-and-the-future-of-the-workforce

Newport, C. (2016). *Deep work: Rules for focused success in a distracted world*. Hachette UK.

Nicolaides, A. (2015). Generative learning: Adults learning within ambiguity. *Adult Education Quarterly, 65*(3), 179–195. http://doi.org/10.1177/0741713614568887

Organization for Economic Cooperation and Development (OECD) (2019). *OECD skills outlook 2019: Thriving in a digital world*. http://doi.org/10.1787/df80bc12-en

Park, Y. J. (1990). Korean patterns of women's labor force participation during the period 1960–1980. *Korea Journal of Population and Development, 19*(1), 71–90.

Peters, M. A. (2020). Beyond technological unemployment: the future of work. *Educational philosophy and theory, 52*(5), 485–491. https://doi.org/10.1080/00131857.2019.1608625

Remus, D., & Levy, Frank S. (2016). *Can robots be lawyers? Computers, lawyers, and the practice of law*. Available at SSRN: https://ssrn.com/abstract=2701092

Rosenblat, A. (2018). *Uberland: How algorithms are rewriting the rules of work*. University of California Press.

Rosenbloom, R. S. (2000). Leadership, capabilities, and technological change: The transformation of NCR in the electronic era. *Strategic Management Journal, 21*(10–11), 1083–1103.

Schwab, K. (2017). *The fourth industrial revolution*. Portfolio Penguin.

Smith, D. W. (2011). Deleuze and the question of desire: Towards an immanent theory of ethics. In N. Jun & D. W. Smith (Eds.), *Deleuze and ethics* (pp. 123–141). Edinburgh University Press

Stiegler, B. (2019). For a neganthropology of automatic society. In T. Pringle, G. Koch, & B. Stiegler (Eds.), *Machine (In Search of Media)*, pp. 25–48. Meson Press.

Tambe, P., Cappelli, P., & Yakubovich, V. (2019). Artificial intelligence in human resources management: Challenges and a path forward. *California Management Review, 61*(4), 15–42. https://doi.org/10.1177/0008125619867910

Taylor, M. C. (2020). *Intervolution: Smart bodies smart things*. Columbia University Press.

Thurow, L. C. (1999). *Creating wealth: The new rules for individuals, companies and countries in a knowledge-based economy.* Granite Hill Publishers.

Torbert, W. R. (2004). *Action inquiry: The secret of timely and transforming leadership.* Berrett-Koehler Publishers.

Tuck, E., & Yang, K. W. (2014). R-words: Refusing research. *Humanizing Research: Decolonizing Qualitative Inquiry with Youth and Communities, 223.* https://dx.doi.org/10.4135/9781544329611.n12

Wergin, J. F. (2019). *Deep learning in a disorienting world.* Cambridge University Press

World Economic Forum (2016). *The 10 skills you need to thrive in the Fourth Industrial Revolution.* Retrieved October 20, 2019, from https://www.weforum.org/agenda/2016/01/the-10-skills-you-need-to-thrive-in-the-fourth-industrial-revolution/

EIGHT

 The Dynamics of Generative Learning

THIS BOOK IS WRITTEN PHENOMENOLOGICALLY, in that how you do generative learning and how generative knowing emerges are the stuff of each chapter. To facilitate generative learning, you have to create spaces of possibility. Each chapter in this book is a space of possibility. Spaces of possibility are places (imagined and real) filled with the unconventional entanglement of lived experiences that are alive in the past, present, and emerging future. Ontology, the dynamics of reality, is not bound by time and space, and being is unfolding in ways that become knowing in service of vitalizing self and society; they need each other. Generative knowing animates adult learning by attending to the dynamics of reality (ontology), knowing (epistemology), actualizing potential (axiology), and societal vision (self and society) that form ethical response-ability (Pratt, 1998; Ross, 2021). Generative knowing: ways of being and becoming, actualizes potential, creatively making self and society vital. Making learning vital, just in time to activate a response-ability to the next cycle of disquiet that people and the planet face. Self and society need each other to find a way to navigate the fluid territory of complexity.

A Nomadic Theory of Adult Learning

Nomads in colloquial vernacular denote a wandering kind of approach to living, as if land and home do not belong to a nomad. Philosophically, nomadic signals the fluid and intra-active relatedness of self and society. Nomadic implies the all-ready entangled learning leaving no-one-no-thing behind. A no-center reality of a living life that is bound by more than land and home. Evolving a nomadic adult learning theory is an act of making manifest a truth of learning that is shy, vulnerable, and prefers the slow luminous darkness where being is all-ready and not-yet. A nomad is humble, living in the space of possibility following the lines of sand, salt, and roots that reveal the stuff of life. From the margins, a nomad knows limitations: limitations of life constructed for some to keep home and land intact, while for others a life tossed up in the air, daring survival. Nomads know where to find water and how water is poisoned at the well; they know that humility is the only disposition of self that forges spaces for possibility. The space for new worlds. Nomads receive, return, respond to all that is given. A knowing that mystery is generous in spite of our limitations to know mystery. The stories I have shared with you are stories of nomads, the being and becoming of people who have been erased, stories that are not to be told, stories better kept hidden and/or secret, new story making. The stuff of these stories is the material for generative knowing to make things different. To actualize potential, creatively making self and society a better fit: a fit for many ways of being and becoming that generative knowing makes.

I think of adult learning as the potency of transformation. We are living in a time between two worlds (Stein, 2019), when transformation is all-ready and not-yet. A space that contains the potential for a world struggling to become. This space is a fitting landscape for generative knowing to emerge. As I write this final chapter, I am living in a global moment that is not entirely unfamiliar to me or to you, the reader. An ongoing Global Pandemic; the evisceration of a self-determined society—currently Ukraine; the genocide of people who are different—most recently the Rohingya of Myanmar; the climate crisis that is having multiple impacts such as rising water levels, the warming of coral reefs in Australia, and environmental migrants in search of potable water, to name but a few in the recent news. The unfolding of life evolving gets snagged from time to time when the confluence of experiences overwhelms, activating well-worn habits of looking away or falling back for escape or solutions that colonize self and society, keeping vitality stagnant (Livesay, 2013; McCallum, 2008). Looking away and/or falling back are the tools of colonialization, re-producing the known and privileged reality that a portion of humanity clings to, using knowing to keep reality where it is rather than allowing for something different to emerge. The power of re-production keeps self and society blind to the potential of something different. Only when these entanglements get tangled in such profound ways do they become signals that something different is possible, that potential is waiting to be perceived, opening portals to new worlds becoming. These portals are hard to see and always in the blind spots of self and society, where mystery hosts spaces of possibility. When we collectively turn away from experience and the sensations that accompany such experiences, we also lose the opportunity to perceive the emergence of potential that could make things different. Seeing in the dark awakens mystery, making it possible to trust and be held by the unknown, a generosity that welcomes potential.

Generative knowing is a new beginning, an opening. Its purpose is to make things different together. Making things different together is radical—radical in that truth, justice, and beauty become real as acts of response-ability. Vitalizing potential to become something new is what generative knowing does. Making new worlds is hard work. It has limitations in that its rhythms are unpredictable, requiring both constraints and freedoms for emergence to configure something different. Generative knowing is humble, shy, vulnerable in an open state of relatedness that receives sensations without shying away. Not shying away is a radical act of learning that is generative.

Making things different together creatively is what generative knowing does. Generative knowing does this by evolving ways of being and becoming activating potential for response-ability in self and society. That is what making means, to make something different real. Something different connotes vital new worlds that cannot be fore-known and are all-ready. Vital new worlds are the stuff of transformations, transformations that are in a state of not-yet. Becoming is how potential is vitalized when we experience the experience of experience and the sensations that accompany it, unfurling generative knowing and activating potential creatively; making new worlds. Sensations are the language of generative knowing, more like symbols than instructions, more like tickles than shocks. Following these sensations demands that learning begins with being, not doing, not action. It is in the being that generative knowing is catalyzed, making possible new ways of becoming that shape response-ability. Response-ability is the act, the doing of generative knowing, making things different that begins beneath in the territory of the dynamics of reality.

The Dynamics of Generative Learning

Generative knowing is a languaging (Maturana, 1988) of adult learning that seeks to grow and evolve ways of being and becoming that make ethical response possible. Actualizing potential in ways that vitalize human being and becoming is a much-needed global moral resource for making new worlds.

The inquiry that holds this book together, "How do we build a just and equitable society to which to all of us can belong?" is an inquiry without an ending. It is an inquiry that catalyzes our imagination deeper and wider in the making of words that fit all, us, human and more-than-human dynamic realities.

How Can Adult Educators Facilitate This Way of Knowing?

I am an adult educator, aware that not all learning needs to be or wants to be generative. Most of my graduate students want learning that is knowable in ways with which they are familiar. Familiarity is a tool of adult learning that makes knowledge known through skillful curating of content, knowledge of adult learning styles, presentation of key concepts, and the cultivation of understanding, so that students can go and learn some more. Learning more is a tricky idea in that learning more is dangerously close to doing more learning. It is like filling a cup that is already full. Learning more is useful when knowledge is sought to solve a problem that is recognizable. Learning more is an excellent approach to gaining mastery of concepts. Learning more is a brilliant approach to apprenticeship models of adult learning. However, learning more to respond to challenges such as making reality different is not as good a fit. The misfit of learning more and cultivating response-ability is like the Janus relationship of science and mystery. Both are needed in some elegant balance that emerges beautifully when the conditions, internal and external, are ready.

To be an adult educator who also develops the capacity for generative knowing requires at least three internal dispositions:

- Resonant Intimacy: A commitment to the unfolding mystery of knowing that emerges through inquiry.
- Courageous Vulnerability: A capacity for frame-breaking with humility of putting at risk what is known.
- Flexible Emergence: A joyful surprise that arises when making things different.

These three dispositions are not learned in the conventional sense; they are a way of being in relationship to the many potentials that learning can become; dispositions that are cultivated over a lifetime of curiosity and a willingness to try making new things with learning. Generative knowing is likened to the education as liberation that Freire cultivated for freedom from oppression. Generative knowing makes teaching, leading learning, a process to awaken students' values and ideologies, to make them an object of critical reflection, to become curious about what learning creates if it does not create the possibility for all beings regardless of power, privilege, race, ethnicity, access, and all the ways that learning serves to exclude and reproduce (Pratt, 1998). To make different worlds. These dispositions create the internal conditions for spaces of possibility (Juarrero, 2002): spaces of possibility where generative knowing emerges as ways of being and becoming, creatively activating potential.

Creating spaces of possibility for generative knowing to emerge requires three external scaffolds:

- Designed Constraints: A space that is free of judgment, cultivates authentic dialogue, looks and feels like a space for learning. Where catalysts, feedback loops, and resonance are embodied. Where response-ability emerges from beneath experience (bottom-up) as an act of potential.
- Spacious Freedoms: A space where all learning is welcome, including informational, instrumental, transformational, that makes way for generative knowing to emerge. The use of narrative, storytelling, and re-story(ing) that move across time and space (past, present, and future) in surprising ways makes many possibilities real.
- Thriving Complexity: A space where interdependence is alive. Tending to relationships to self, each other, and the larger context that is always dynamic. Paying attention across boundaries with care and curiosity. Working with what is known and not fore-knowable. The whole and parts in dynamic play, making new realities from unexpected collisions.

Cultivating capacity for generative knowing is a mutual affair. The educator cultivates the interior dispositions, evolves ways to create spaces for possibility where intra-actions are free to roam. Students (adult learners) bring their desire for learning that begins with being, something that is at first awkward. A mutual trust arises by practicing together with the aspects of generative knowing. By "together," I mean that in spaces of possibility everyone is learning in a way that is not fore-known. When this becomes real, with everyone learning in a deliberate space of possibility, the potential for generative knowing to emerge is activated. The aspects of generative knowing discussed in this book are:

- *Ruptures*: An encounter with the unknown that undergoing an experience of experience brings in the form of sensations.
- *In-scending*: To listen into the dark. To inquire in the territory beneath the experience of experience. To receive the sensations.
- *Awaring*: The creative activation of potential as ways of being and becoming. Making different worlds real. Receiving the grace of the sensations.

These aspects are the content of cultivating the capacity for response-ability. The ethical action that emerges from beneath experience as we undergo it. Ethics here refers to the affirmative potential that is catalyzed through generative knowing, a grace given from mystery. Ethics and mystery go hand in hand, getting learning into trouble. Troubling learning is to recognize that learning has played its role at holding mystery at bay in service of colonizing worldviews that keep things in place. Fascism is learning holding mystery at bay, a turning away from multiple truths, fixating on one privileged illusion. Transformation is the stuff of learning when mystery is in conversation with the intra-active dynamics of reality, beneath experience, in the sensations of experience that activate many potentials. Many potentials are the stuff of ethics (Braidotti, 2019) that emerge in ways of being and becoming as generative knowing.

Self and Society

Adult learning in this time between worlds re-turns us to imagine the thick flows of potential that are the stuff of self and society. A relatedness that is not separate, as I have discussed throughout this book, along with many adult educators before me—such as Heron, 1992; Freire, 1970; Jarvis, 1992, 2011; and Mezirow, 1978, to name a few. Ambiguity is the currency of self and society. A not fore-known, all-ready and not-yet dynamic reality that emerges as generative knowing guides response-ability. As an adult educator I am challenged to create spaces of possibility as a response to the complexity we are in together, and yet not the same. My desire is for this book to serve as a portal into many spaces of possibility. That generative knowing is received as a way to unfold and make real the being and becoming of learning, inviting different rhythms for creative potential to take shape. These new rhythms of learning begin with *Ruptures* in the way self and society are known. Seeing the *Ruptures* for what they are, that is, signals to perceive a territory that cannot be fore-known, a first aspect of generative knowing. Accepting that we do not know, the unknown is the languaging of *Ruptures*. *Ruptures* are the first invitation into the mystery, a territory that draws you in beneath its fertile territory, where potential is in a state of not-yet, rich compost for generative knowing to emerge. To activate the potential for multiple ways of being and becoming, *In-scending* is a practice of following the sensations of experience, to undergo them, inquiring into the invisible world beneath experience, a deeper aspect of generative knowing. In the depth of this territory, there is nothing known; the rhythm of learning is slow, shy, vulnerable, and luminous in the darkness. Seeing in the dark is a process of *Awaring* the sensations, symbols, truth(s) that emerge from the invisible world of experience, that cannot be fore-known. *Awaring* the gifts given that emerge from the intra-active play of mystery and grace in-forms ethical response-ability. Actualizing ethical response-ability makes potential real, making things different, new worlds together. New worlds need self and society to become real in their all-ready interdependence. An entanglement that brings new worlds into being.

References

Freire, P. (1970). *Pedagogy of the oppressed*. Herder and Herder.
Heron, J. (1992). *Feeling and personhood: Psychology in another key*. Sage.
Heron, J. (1996). *Co-operative inquiry: Research into the human condition*. Sage.
Jarvis, P. (1992). *Paradoxes of learning: On becoming an individual in society*. Wiley.
Jarvis, P. (2011). *Teaching, learning and education in late modernity: The selected works of Peter Jarvis* (1st ed.). Routledge. https://doi.org/10.4324/9780203802946
Juarrero, A. (2002). *Dynamics in action: Intentional behavior as a complex system*. MIT Press.
Livesay, V. T. (2013). *Exploring the paradoxical role and experience of fallback in developmental theory*. [Doctoral dissertation, University of San Diego].
Maturana, H. R. (1988). Reality: The search for objectivity or the quest for a compelling argument. *Irish Journal of Psychology, 9*(1), 25–82. https://doi.org/10.1080/03033910.1988.10557705

McCallum, D. C., Jr. (2008). *Exploring the implications of a hidden diversity in Group Relations Conference learning: A developmental perspective.* [Doctoral dissertation, Teachers College, Columbia University]. Retrieved from http://proquest.umi.com/pqdweb?did=1601316511&Fmt=7&clientId=28362&RQT=309&VName=PQD

Mezirow, J. (1978). Perspective Transformation. *Adult Education Quarterly, 28*(2), 100–110. https://doi.org/10.1177/074171367802800202

Mezirow, J. (1991). *Transformative dimensions of adult learning.* ERIC.

Mezirow, J. (2000). *Learning as transformation: Critical perspectives on a theory in progress.* Wiley.

Pratt, D. D. and Associates. (1998). *Five perspectives on teaching in adult and higher education.* Krieger Publishing.

Ross, E. K. (2021). *Transforming the ways we create change: Experiencing and cultivating transformative sustainability learning.* [Doctoral dissertation, University of Technology, Sydney].

Stein, Z. (2019). *Education in a time between worlds: Essays on the future of schools, technology, and society.* Bright Alliance.

About the Authors

Aliki Nicolaides EdD, is Associate Professor of Adult Learning, Leadership and Adult Development at the University of Georgia in the program of Learning, Leadership and Organization Development. Dr. Nicolaides seeks to optimize vital developmental conditions for adults, groups and systems to learn and grow. Through the past decade of research and teaching, she has developed a philosophy of adult learning, Generative Knowing. This philosophy highlights and explores how adults learn their way through the complexity and ambiguity that is so prevalent in this period of "liquid" modernity. Specifically, her work suggests that under certain conditions and with intentional scaffolding, encounters with ambiguity and complexity can evoke deep learning and reveal hidden potential that generates response-able, knowing and action. Dr. Nicolaides' facilitation approach is grounded in Collaborative Developmental Action Inquiry (CDAI); a methodology which consciously develops adults' intra-and-inter active capacity to respond to the fluidity of the 21st century lifeworld. The complex demands of a rapidly changing, interconnected world require new ways in knowing and being in the world.

Generative Knowing and CDAI undergird her teaching, scholarship and practice philosophy, catalyzing conditions for adult's learning that actualized multiple potentials as response to complexity and uncertainty that connect us across cultural and ethical contexts. In addition to her academic scholarship and facilitation, Dr. Nicolaides is a founding steward and current Director of the International Transformative Learning Association. The purpose of the association is to promote global critical scholarship, research, teaching, application, and praxis of the social, scientific, artistic, and humanistic principles of transformative learning theories and praxis.

Now retired, **Elizabeth Kasl** taught doctoral students about transformative learning at Teachers College, Columbia University and California Institute of Integral Studies. She focused on collaborative learning, participatory inquiry, the role of diversity in knowledge construction, whole-person epistemology, and holism in pedagogical practice. She helped create three small group learning collaboratives. The last group, European-American Collaborative Challenging Whiteness, was founded in 1997 and continues to this day.

Ahreum Lim is a Ph.D. candidate in Learning, Leadership, and Organization Development at the University of Georgia (UGA). Broadly conceived, her doctoral work is an inquiry into the generative role of adult learning in the context of the future of work where advanced technology putatively affects the agency of the human workforce. She is working on her dissertation in collaboration with the engineering education lab to develop inquiry-based training for future engineers using the generative knowing theory.

Index

1997 Asian Financial Crisis, 113
1998 U.N. Commission on Human Rights, 85
#MeToo, 51, 52

A
action logic, 20
actual, 122
actualized, 122
adaptive learning, 19
adult learning
    brief review of, 13–16
    concepts in dialogue, 16–25
    evolving, 24–25
    experience of experience and, 69
    familiarity and, 132
    as a force of change, 66
    generative knowing and, 66
    good trouble and, 5–6
    languaging and, 131
    lineage of, 3–4
    nomadic theory of, xxvi, 1–3, 6–9, 25–26, 70, 129–31
    personal and societal belonging and, xxiv
    as potency of transformation, 130
    reorienting desire and, 116
    Also see generative learning
aesthetics, 35
affirmative ethics, 7
agency, 59–60, 61
Ahenakew, C., 89
Ahmed, A., 5,
Ahmed, S., 88
Alchemist, 20, 22
algorithms, 116, 117, 121
Alhadeff-Jones, M., 7, 14
Allen, P., 34
all-ready, 66, 86
Alverson, M., 47
Alvesson, M., 70
ambiguity, xxiii, 1–2, 9, 20, 47–49, 54, 134
    author's encounters with, 36
    complexity and, 35
    conversations about, 36–37
    danger and mystery of, 43
    integrity and, 38–42
    learning within, 44–46

murky use of language, 42
mutuality and, 42–44
origins of term, 29
pandemic life and, 87
pursuit of, 38
three-act play and, 31–34
vulnerability, intimacy and, 39
American Pragmatism, 4, 15
Anderson, T., 113
Anderson, W., 124
Anthropocene, 118
Arab Israeli War, xxi
Argyris, C., 20, 21
Art as Experience, 15, 68
artificial intelligence, 117
Atkinson, P., 46
awareness, 48
Awaring, xxv, 8, 48, 51, 66, 100, 134, 135
axiology, 129

B
Bachelard, 30
Balfour Declaration, 90
Bandura, A., 59
Bang, H., 112
Barad, K., xxiv, 2, 5, 13, 15, 52
Barry, A., 24
Bateson, G., 7, 16, 17, 19, 21, 22, 23, 24, 104, 106, 107, 108, 116, 121, 123
Bauman, Z., 5, 35
Baumgartner, L.M., 17
becoming, 2, 8, 66, 99
becoming nomadic, 7
being, 66, 99
Benavente, B.R., 6
Benson, K., 70
Benz, V.H., 36
Berkowitz, R., 107
Bogue, R., 119
Bohr, N., 51
Boone, M.E., 35
Boulton, J., 34
Bourdieu, P., 38
Boyatzis, R.E., 105
Braidotti, R., 5, 6, 7, 8, 13, 108, 116, 118, 119, 122, 124, 134

Bridle, J., 104
British Mandate, 87, 88, 90, 94, 95
Brookfield, S., 3, 5
Broussard, M., 104, 117, 118, 120
Brown, J.S., xxv, 8, 18
Brown, L., 124
Brynjolfsson, E., 122
Buddhism, xxiii
Butler, J., 5

C
California Institute of Integral Studies, xix
capacity, 18
cartography, 58–59, 89
cartography of terror, 58–59
ceasing-to-be, 124
certainty, 1, 2
Charmaz, K., 46
chatbot technology, 105
Chiva, R., 19, 21
Choi, T., 114
Chopard, K., 77
Chung, J., 114
Cilliers, P., 34
cognitive sciences, 6
collaborative developmental action inquiry (CDAI), 23
collaborative learning, xx
communion, 71
competency modeling, 105, 106
complex ways of knowing, doing, and being, 34
complexity, xxiv, 34
    ambiguity and, 35
complexity science, xxiii, 35
complex singularity, 109
conceptual persona, 119, 122
constructive development theory, xxiii
constructivist epistemology, 17
constructivism, 3, 13, 17
conversation, 31, 34, 38
    murky use of language, 42
    reflexive, 47
Cook-Greuter, S.R., 22, 34
Courageous Vulnerability, 132
Crawford, K., 104
cultural philosophy, xxv, 9
cybernetic representation, 121

D
d'Agnese, V., 14, 15, 107

Dahlberg, H., 36
Dahlberg, K., 36
Daloz, L.A., 16, 66
Danaher, J., 104, 118, 120, 122
Davis, J.H., 36
decolonial gesture, 89
decolonizing movements, 88
deep inquiry, 77
deep learning, 1
deep practice of inquiry, 78
Deleuze, G., xxv, 2, 4, 7, 19, 24, 25, 59, 77–78, 107, 119, 120, 121, 122, 123
Deloitte Global, 118
deMarrais, K., 46
Democracy and Education, 15
Derrida, J., 60
Designed Constraints, 133
desire, 107
deterritorialization, 19, 59
deuteron-learning, 21
Dewey, J., xxv, 1, 3, 4, 5, 6, 9, 13, 14, 15, 52, 68, 103, 104, 107, 114, 115, 122
diffraction, 6
diffractive analysis, 5, 6
discomfort, 89
displaced persons, 85, 88
doing, 103–4, 105–7
double-loop learning, 20, 23
downloading, 21

E
educational psychology, 17
ego awareness, 22
Elias, J.L., 3, 5
embodied reflexivity, 70, 71
epistemology, 16, 129
Eshenbacher, S., 3
ethics, 134
European-American Collaborative Challenging Whiteness, xx
evocation, 14
evolutionary biology, xxiii
evolving, 4–5
existence, 52
experience of experience, 69, 103
experience, nature of, 15–16, 68–72

F
Fascism, 134
felt-sense, xxvi

Index

Fenwick, T.J., 6, 17, 18, 35
Finnegan, F., 3
Fleming, T., 3
Flexible Emergence, 132
Follett, M.P., 6, 7, 13, 14, 15, 16
forced ambiguity, xvii
fourth industrial revolution, 122
Freeman, M., 20, 31
Freire, P., 4, 16, 134
Futures of Education: Learning to Become, xxv

G

Gadamer, J., 30, 31
Gay, R., 65
Gebser, J., xxv, 4, 9
Gendlin, E.T., xxvi
generational trauma, 87
generative ambiguity, xxiii
generative knowing, xviii, xix, xxiv–xxv, 4, 51–54, 60–61, 134
   adult learning and, 66
   Awaring and, 100
   commodification and instrumentalization of learning and, 119
   deep inquiry and, 77–78
   definition of, xvi, 2
   fluid allowing and, 67
   freedom and, 71
   future of work and, 103–4, 116–22
   languaging and, 54, 131
   listening to stories, 35
   as a nomadic theory, 5–6, 25–26
   not foreknowable and, 51
   Ruptures and, 80–81
   reterritorialization and, 59
   socio-technical complexity and, 103
   three external scaffolds for, 133
   three internal dispositions required, 132–33
   Also see generative learning
generative learning, xxvi, 1–3
   aspects of, 8–9
   boundaries of experience and, 59
   cognitive sciences and, 6
   definition, 18
   dynamics of, 129, 131–35
   educational psychology and, 17
   four processes for, 17
   organizational learning and, 19
   triple-loop learning and, 6, 20–24
   Also see generative knowing
Giddens, A., 38
Gillespie, T., 117
Gilligan, C., 4
Grbich, C., 46
Greene, M., 7
Griffin, D., 34
Group for Collaborative Inquiry, xx
Guattari, F., xxv, 2, 4, 7, 19, 24, 25, 59, 77–78, 107, 119, 120, 121, 122, 123

H

Habermas, J., 19
Habib, J., 19, 21
habitual thinking, 121, 122
hagwans, 113, 114
Haigh, T., 118
Haraway, D., 59, 89
Harvey, S.W., 36
Heidegger, M., 121
Hendry, P., 70
Heron, J., 5, 18, 134
Hesse-Biber, S.N., 70
Hoggan, C.D., 69
Hom, P.W., 105
hooks, b., 5
Horton, M., 4
Hua, C.B., 76
human-centeredness, 117
human-machine interaction, 103
human-more-than-human-ambiguity, 1, 2
humanism, 3, 13
human-ness, 116–17
Hunter, A., 39

I

individual consciousness, xix
In-scending, 8, 48, 51, 57, 66, 69, 70, 71–72, 77, 87, 134
instrumentalized learning, 106
interconnection, xxiv
International Labor Organization, 118
International Transformative Learning Conference, xv
inter-subjective meaning-making, 36
intra-action, 60, 70, 71, 85
intra-active forces, 58
invisible, 66
invisible world, 1

J

James, W., 4
Jarvis, P., 3, 5, 66, 134

job analysis, 105
"jobless" capitalist society, 107
Johnson, J., xxv, xxvi, 4, 9
Jones, R.S., 113
justice, 60

K
Kasl, E., xx
Katz, C., 26
Kegan, R., 3, 4, 21, 34, 35, 116
Kim, J.-S., 112
Kimmerer, R.W., 5
knowing
    multiple ways of, 3
    theory of, 68–69
knowledge construction, xx
Knowles, M., 4
Kohlberg, L., 5
Kohler, H.P., 113
Kolb, D.A., 103
Korea University, 113
Kuhn, A., 70
Kwon, C., 20, 22

L
languaging, 54
Lawrence-Lightfoot, S., 36
learning
    commodification and instrumentalization of, 119
    controlled activity and, 115
    definition of, 3
    due process and, 116
    future of work and, 120
    instrumentalized, 106
    troubling, 134
learning about, 8
learning-from-ambiguity, 1
learning how, xix
Learning Level I, 19, 21, 22
Learning Level II, 19, 22, 108
Learning Level III, 21, 22, 23, 24
Learning Level IV, 21
learning that, xix
learning through ambiguity, xvi
learning to be, 8
learning to become, xix, 8
Lee, J.K., 113
Lee, S., 124
Leng, L.Y., 76

Levy, F.S., 117
Lewis, J., 5
liberatory education, 19
Lim, A., xxiii, xxvi, 3, 4, 5, 8, 17, 103
Lindell, H., 124
Lindeman, E., 4
Livesay, V.T., 130
Logic: The Theory of Inquiry, 68
Lorde, A., 5, 65
Luttrell, W., 70

M
machinic age, 122
Madison, G.B., 36, 38
Magician, 20, 22
Mälkki, K., xxvi
Marboeuf, O., 89
Marsick, J., xxvi, 72
material-semiotic generative nodes, 59
Mathison, J., 21, 22, 23
matterings, 2
Maturana, H.R., 13, 54, 131
Maxwell, J.A., 36
Mayer, R.E., 17
Mazzei, L.A., 5, 6
McAfee, A., 122
McCallum, D., 18, 22, 23, 34, 130
McClelland, D.C., 105
McGuire, J., 48
McKinsey Global Institute, 118
meaning-making, 18
Melacarne, C., 8, 18, 19
Merleau-Ponty, M., 30, 38
Merriam, S.B., 3, 5, 17
Mezirow, J., xviii, xix, 3, 5, 69, 134
Mikecz, R., 35, 36, 39, 42, 44
Miracle on the Han River, 113
mother nature, 85–90, 90–99, 99–101
Moustakas, C.E., 48
multiplicity, xxiv, 69
mutual inquiry, 42
mutuality, 42, 44
    co-creation and co-generation of, 45
mystery, 134
mystical teaching, xxiii

N
Nabka, xxi, 85
narrative, 46
narrative inquiry, 46

Index

Newport, C., 121
Nicolaides, Aliki (author), xxi, xxiii, xxiv, xxvi, 1, 3, 4, 5, 8, 13, 15, 16, 17, 18, 19, 20, 22, 23, 30, 34, 54, 69, 71, 72, 116, 121
   background of, xxi–xxii
   COVID-19 and, 86–86
   cultural background of, 108
   education of, xxii–xxiii, 109–14
   first, second and third person experiences and, 53
   from survival to generativity, 114–16
   future-self of, 108
   generative knowing of self, 52–53
   hagwans and, 113, 114
   In-scending and, 51, 57
   learning through complexity, 54
   path of inquiry and, 53–54
   as program designer, xxii
   relationship to learning, 123–24
   terror and, 55–56, 58–61
   traumatic experience of, 51, 56–57
   various identities of, 55, 57
   Workforce Development and Vocational Education Program and, 105–7, 115
Nicolaides, Ari
   as a displaced person, 85–90
   employment of, 109–11, 113–14
   mother nature and, 85–90, 90–99, 99–101
   parenting of daughters, 112
Nicolaides, Martha, 63–66
   background of, 63–65
   employment of, 109, 111–12, 113–14
   as a feminist, 65
   parenting of daughters, 112
   Six-Day War and, 65, 66, 67–68, 71, 72–77, 77–78, 78–80
Nicolaides, Theodore, 93
Ninos, T., 93
no longer, 7
nomads, 129–30
nomadic theory, xxvi, 1–3, 6–9, 25–26, 66, 70, 129–31
nomadic thinking, 7
not-yet, 7, 8, 66
not-yet-actualized, 122, 123
not-yet-to-be, 124

O

O'Donohue, J., 1
ontology, 23, 129
ontology as subjective-objective, 18
ontology of the not-foreknown, 29
Organization for Economic Cooperation and Development, 118
organizational learning, 19

P

Palaganas, E.C., 71
Park, Y.J., 111
participative inquiry, xx
Pendleton-Julian, A., xxv, 18
Perry, S., 124
Perry Jr., W.G., 5
personal learning, xviii
perspective transformation, xviii
Peschl, M.F., 20, 23, 24
Peters, M.A., 107
phenomenological data reduction methods, 46–47
phenomenological interviews, xxiii
phenomenological research, 29–34
phenomenological texts, 30
phenomenology, 37
phenomenology of consciousness, xxv, 9
Piercy, F.P., 70
Plesner, U., 42, 44
poestas, 119
Polanyi, M., 4, 8
post-human, 119, 122
potential, 119
power, xvii, 86, 87, 88, 96
pragmatism, xxiii, 3, 13
Pratt, D.D., 129, 133

Q

quantum theory, xxiii, xxiv
Quest for Certainty, The, 68

R

reading as an intentional practice, xviii
reality, 37–38, 72
Reason, P., 18
reflection, 107
reflexivity, 70–71
Remus, D., 117
Resonant Intimacy, 132
response-ability, 60
responsibility, 60
reterritorialization, 19, 59
robocene, 118, 122

Rogers, C., 16
Rorty, R., 5
Rosenblat, A., 104, 117, 120
Rosenbloom, R.S., 111
Ross, E.K., 129
Ruptures, 8, 51, 69, 134
Ruptures in knowing, 48

S
Scharmer, C.O., 5, 13, 19, 21, 23
Schon, D.A., 20
Scully-Russ, E., 5
Schwab, K., 104, 122
self and society, 129, 134–35
Semetsky, 15
Seoul National University, 113
Shapiro, J.J., 36
Shaw, P., 34
Siemens, G., 5
single-loop learning, 20, 22, 23
Six-Day War, xxi, xxvi, 65, 66, 67–68, 71, 72–77, 77–78, 78–80, 85
Skoildberg, K., 47, 70
SKY universities, 113
Snowden, D.J., 35
social cartographies, 89
social movement learning, 3
social network learning, 3
socio-technical complexity, 103
Somerville, M., 70
South Korea
    economic growth, 112–13
    education system, 112–13
    hagwans and, 113
space of the unknown, xxii
spaces of possibility, 129, 133
Spacious Freedoms, 133
Spivak, G.C., 88, 89
Stacey, R., 34
Starr, A., 20
Stein, S., 88
Stein, Z., 130
Stiegler, B., 120, 124
structures of power, 19
systemic stupidity, 124

T
Tambe, P., 117
Taylor, M.C., 121
Teachers College, Columbia University, xix

technology, 116
    online predictions about, 118
    posthuman predicament, 116
    racial bias and, 117
    shortcomings of, 117
    Workforce Development and Vocational Education Program and, 105–7, 115
    Also see work, future of
Theory U, 23
Thomas, D., 8
Thriving Complexity, 133
Thurow, L.C., 118
Ticineto-Clough, P., 78
Tobias, S., 17
Torbert, W.R., 13, 17, 18, 20, 23, 24, 34, 35, 108, 116
Tosey, P., 17, 20, 21, 22, 23
transformation, 130, 134
transformative knowing, xv
transformative learning, 3, 5
Transformative Learning Collaborative, xx
triple-loop learning, 6, 17, 20–24, 108
    three conceptualizations of, 20–21
Tuck, E., 109
tuft of grass, 16

U
undergoing, 14, 15, 103–4
undergoing experience, 4, 69, 122
understanding, 69
UNESCO, xxv, 4
University of Georgia, 103
unknown, 2, 103

V
Van Manen, M., 30, 36
Verela, F.J., 13, 54
Vettraino, E., 70, 71
virtual, 122
volatility, uncertainty, complexity, and ambiguity (VUCA), 18
Vygotsky, L.S., 4, 16

W
Wergin, J.F., 121
within-the-ambiguous, 34
Wittrock, 5, 16, 17
work, future of, 103–4, 105–7, 107–9, 115–16, 116–22
World Economic Forum, 118

Index

Y
Yakoub, J.B., 89
Yang, K.W., 109
Yew, L.K., 67
Yonsei University, 113
Yorks, L., xxiv, 15, 17, 18

Z
zero learning, 19, 21
Zionism, 87